S0-BZE-337

Reading & Understanding
Poems

LEVEL II

About the Cover and the Artist

The design on the cover of this book is a quilt called Contained Crazy Quilt, *created by internationally known quilt artist Jan Myers of Minneapolis, Minnesota. Jan is represented in many corporate and private collections, and in the permanent textiles collection of the Minneapolis Institute of Arts.*

Books in the Program

Short Stories, Level I
    Hardcover Edition
    Teacher's Guide

Nonfiction, Level I
    Hardcover Edition
    Teacher's Guide

Plays, Level I
    Hardcover Edition
    Teacher's Guide

Poems, Level I
    Hardcover Edition
    Teacher's Guide

Short Stories, Level II
    Hardcover Edition
    Teacher's Guide

Nonfiction, Level II
    Hardcover Edition
    Teacher's Guide

Plays, Level II
    Hardcover Edition
    Teacher's Guide

Poems, Level II
    Hardcover Edition
    Teacher's Guide

JAMESTOWN LITERATURE PROGRAM
Growth in Comprehension & Appreciation

Reading & Understanding
Poems

LEVEL II

JAMESTOWN PUBLISHERS

a division of NTC/CONTEMPORARY PUBLISHING GROUP
Lincolnwood, Illinois USA

JAMESTOWN LITERATURE PROGRAM
Growth in Comprehension & Appreciation
Reading & Understanding Poems
LEVEL II

Developed by Jamestown Editorial Group
and Helena Frost Associates

Cover and text design: Deborah Hulsey Christie

Illustrations:
   Chapter 1, T. Sperling
   Chapter 5, Thomas Malloy
   Chapters 6, 8, 12, J. N. Jones

Photographs:
   Chapter 2, Farrell Grehan, Photo Reserachers, Inc.
   Chapter 3, George H. Harrison from Grant Heilman
   Chapter 3, United Nations: United Nations/M. Guthrie
   Chapter 4, salamander: Hall Harrison from Grant Heilman
   Chapter 4, blossoms: Japan National Tourist Organization
   Chapter 7, Grant Heilman, Lititz, PA
   Chapter 7, "Birches": Photo Researchers
   Chapter 9, Thomas Malloy
   Chapter 10, Paul Conklin/Time Magazine
   Chapter 11, "Song for the Sun . . .": National Oceanic
      and Atmospheric Administration
   Chapter 11, "Clear Evening After Rain": Thomas Nebbia
   Chapter 11, "The Moon Rises": M. C. Escher

ISBN: 0-89061-493-8 (softbound)
ISBN: 0-89061-696-5 (hardbound)

Published by Jamestown Publishers,
a division of NTC/Contemporary Publishing Group, Inc.,
4255 West Touhy Avenue,
Lincolnwood (Chicago), Illinois 60646-1975 U.S.A.

9 0 1 2 3 4 QK 8 7 6 5 4 3 2

Acknowledgments

Acknowledgment is gratefully made to the following individuals and publishers for permission to reprint the works of the authors appearing in this book.

"Recuerdo" by Edna St. Vincent Millay. From *Complete Poems,* Harper & Row. Copyright © 1922, 1950 by Edna St. Vincent Millay. Reprinted by permission.

"Fern Hill" by Dylan Thomas. From *The Poems of Dylan Thomas.* Copyright © 1945 by the Trustees for the copyrights of Dylan Thomas. Reprinted by permission of New Directions Publishing Corporation.

"Pied Beauty" by Gerard Manley Hopkins. From *The Poems of Gerard Manley Hopkins,* published by Oxford University Press for the Society of Jesus.

"may my heart always be open to little" by E. E. Cummings. Copyright © 1938 by E. E. Cummings; renewed 1966 by Marion Morehouse Cummings. Reprinted from *Complete Poems 1913–1962* by permission of Harcourt Brace Jovanovich, Inc.

"Susie Asado" by Gertrude Stein. From *Selected Writings of Gertrude Stein.* Copyright © 1946 by Random House, Inc. Reprinted by permission of the publisher.

"The Chestnut Burr," "Mountain Plum Blossoms," and "Lightning at Night" by Matsuo Basho. From *An Introduction to Haiku* by Harold G. Henderson. Copyright © 1958 by Harold G. Henderson. Reprinted by permission of Doubleday & Company, Inc.

"The Locust Tree in Flower" by William Carlos Williams. From *Collected Poems Volume I: 1909–1939*. Copyright © 1939 by New Directions Publishing Corporation. Reprinted by permission of New Directions Publishing Corporation.

"Living" by Denise Levertov. From *Poems 1960–1967*. Copyright © 1967 by Denise Levertov Goodman. Reprinted by permission of New Directions Publishing Corporation.

"I Am Not Yours" by Sara Teasdale. Reprinted with permission of Macmillan Publishing Company from *Collected Poems* by Sara Teasdale. Copyright © 1915 by Macmillan Publishing Company; renewed 1943 by Mamie T. Wheless.

"Not Waving but Drowning" by Stevie Smith. From *Collected Poems*. Copyright © 1972 by Stevie Smith. Reprinted by permission of New Directions Publishing Corporation.

"The Secret Heart" by Robert P. Tristram Coffin. Reprinted with permission of Macmillan Publishing Company from *Collected Poems* by Robert P. Tristram Coffin. Copyright © 1935 by Macmillan Publishing Company; renewed 1963 by Margaret Coffin Halvosa.

"The Song of Wandering Aengus" by William Butler Yeats. From *The Collected Poems of William Butler Yeats*. Reprinted by permission of A. P. Watt Ltd. on behalf of Michael B. Yeats and Macmillan London Ltd. (Canadian rights). From *The Poems of William Butler Yeats: A New Edition* edited by Richard J. Finneran (New York: Macmillan, 1983).

"Invitation Standing" by Paul Blackburn. Copyright © 1967 by Paul Blackburn.

"I Heard a Fly Buzz" by Emily Dickinson. Reprinted by permission of Harvard University Press and the Trustees of Amherst College. From *The Poems of Emily Dickinson*, edited by Thomas H. Johnson. Cambridge, MA: The Belknap Press of Harvard University Press. Copyright © 1951, 1955, 1979, 1983 by the President and Fellows of Harvard College.

"Birches" by Robert Frost. Copyright © 1916 by Holt, Rinehart & Winston, Inc. Copyright 1944 by Robert Frost. Reprinted from *The Poetry of Robert Frost*, edited by Edward Connery Lathem, by permission of Henry Holt & Company, Inc.

"Heart Crown and Mirror," calligrammes by Guillaume Apollinaire, translated by Kenneth Koch. From *Rose, Where Did You Get That Red?* by Kenneth Koch. Copyright © 1973 by Kenneth Koch. Reprinted by permission of Random House, Inc.

"Blowin' in the Wind" by Bob Dylan. Copyright © 1962 Warner Bros., Inc. All rights reserved. Used by permission.

"Song for the Sun That Disappeared Behind the Rainclouds" by the Khoikhoi (Hottentot) Tribe. From *Rose, Where Did You Get That Red?* by Kenneth Koch. Copyright © 1973 by Kenneth Koch. Courtesy of Random House, Inc.

"Clear Evening After Rain" by Tu Fu. From *One Hundred Poems From the Chinese,* translated by Kenneth Rexroth. Copyright © 1971 by Kenneth Rexroth. All rights reserved. Reprinted by permission of New Directions Publishing Corporation.

"The Moon Rises" by Federico García Lorca. Translated by William B. Logan. From *Selected Poems.* Copyright © 1955 by New Directions Publishing Corporation. Reprinted by permission of New Directions Publishing Corporation.

"From a Childhood" by Rainer Maria Rilke. Reprinted from *Translations from the Poetry of Rainer Maria Rilke* by M. D. Herter Norton, by permission of W. W. Norton & Company, Inc. Copyright renewed 1966 by M. D. Herter Norton.

"Poem: Hate is only one of many responses" by Frank O'Hara. From *The Collected Poems of Frank O'Hara,* edited by Donald Allen. Copyright © 1971 by Maureen Granville-Smith. Reprinted by permission of Alfred A. Knopf, Inc.

Contents

To the Student

Long before poems were ever written, they were sung, chanted, or told as stories with musical accompaniments. In ancient societies poems were part of the everyday oral culture through which people learned about themselves.

Today we usually think of poems in their written form, and we tend to assume that they are difficult to understand. One difficulty we encounter is that we are used to reading prose, and poems look different because they are arranged into lines rather than into paragraphs. Often the language of poetry does not sound like ordinary conversation or read like prose. Yet most poems are not difficult to read or to understand, and they can be as enjoyable as any other kind of literature. In this book you will learn *how* poems are put together and *why* poets write in a particular form. Poets use their imaginations and creative talents to examine feelings, challenges, and issues they see in the world around them.

In this book you will learn how to approach poems as a particularly vivid and compact form of literature. Each chapter contains one or more poems and teaches skills that will help you to interpret the poems. In addition, each chapter begins with About the Selection(s), a section that introduces you to the poem or poems and tells you about the poets who wrote them. Knowing a poet's background often helps you to understand and to appreciate his or her work.

The last feature of the book is a glossary that includes all the literary terms introduced in the book. As you read, you will find several literary terms underlined in each chapter. The first time a term appears in the text, it is underlined and defined. In the glossary, a page reference following each term indicates where the term first appears.

In this book you will find a variety of poems—some serious, others light, some short, others long—that will help you to understand the diverse subjects and the various approaches that poets bring to poetry.

The Sounds
of Poetry

*P*oets are often asked to read or speak lines from their poems before an audience. A poetry reading is very different from a play. Poets are not trained actors, and they do not usually make gestures, wear costumes, or perform in front of scenery. Rather, the purpose of the reading is to allow the audience to hear the sound of the poetry itself, and to focus on the rhythm and flow of the language as well as on the pictures the poem suggests.

Rhythm, or the pattern of sounds, is at the heart of poetry, just as it is in music. In fact, early poetry was closely connected to songs. In primitive societies people rhythmically chanted and sang to the accompaniment of musical instruments. Gradually, those early chants were fashioned into the world's earliest forms of poetry.

Although poetry has deep religious roots, it has also been written about many other subjects. Despite poetry's variations, it has preserved its musical quality. In Unit One you will examine some of the many devices of sound that poets use to create the peaceful, puzzling, startling, or playful sounds in their poems.

Probably the most familiar device of sound associated with poetry is rhyme. Yet many poems use little or no rhyme. Instead, they rely on other patterns and elements.

Listening to the sounds of a poem helps you not only appreciate its melodic qualities but also understand its meaning.

Chapter 1

Selections

Annabel Lee
EDGAR ALLAN POE

Recuerdo
EDNA ST. VINCENT MILLAY

Lesson

Sound in Poetry

About the Selections

As you read in the introduction to Unit One, the first poems were composed thousands of years ago. In ancient times poems were sung to the accompaniment of lyres or other simple stringed instruments. Because of its origins, poetry has always had a musical quality. Many poems have regular rhythm, and the lines flow smoothly from one to the next.

In this chapter you will read two poems: "Annabel Lee" by Edgar Allan Poe and "Recuerdo" (ray-KWAIR-doh) by Edna St. Vincent Millay. What these poems share with each other and with all good poetry is a special kind of verbal music. Poe and Millay use the sounds of words to give the poems a musical quality. That quality is a result of certain elements common to poetry from earliest times: repetition, rhyme, rhythm, and meter. As you will learn, the musicality of any poem can be analyzed in terms of those basic elements.

The musical sound is often what strikes you first about a poem, and it is often what you remember best. The musical quality of a poem supports and reinforces its meaning.

The two poems that you are about to read are about love. However, they approach that subject in very different ways. Edgar Allan Poe's Annabel Lee is dark, tragic, and eerie. The speaker adored a woman "with a love that was more than love," and after her sudden death, he still continues to love her.

By contrast, Edna St. Vincent Millay's "Recuerdo" recalls a joyous, sweet moment in two people's lives. *Recuerdo* is a Spanish word that means "memory" or "remembrance." The speaker in the poem remembers an exhilarating experience in her life which is very different from the sadness of "Annabel Lee." While "Annabel Lee" concerns an attachment so intense that it becomes eternal, "Recuerdo" portrays a fleeting moment of joy, a happy occasion that passed quickly.

Haunted, gloomy, and tormented poems and stories are a trademark of Edgar Allan Poe. He was born in Boston in 1809. His parents were actors who traveled a great deal. At the age of three, after his father deserted the family and his mother died, Poe became an orphan. He was raised by John and Frances Allan, a well-to-do couple whose name Poe later added to his own.

In 1826 Poe entered the University of Virginia. Although he did well in his studies, he ran up more debts than John Allan was willing to pay, and after one semester Poe was forced to leave. He then joined the army and eventually received an appointment to West Point. At West Point, however, Poe changed his mind about a military career. He stopped going to classes and was finally expelled. He was then twenty-two years old.

For the remaining eighteen years of his life, Poe worked as an editor and critic. He wrote articles, stories, and poems for various magazines. He had some success as a writer and editor but he never earned very much. Consequently, Poe and his wife lived in near poverty.

Poe's life was complicated by worries about his wife, Virginia, whom he married in 1836. She was an invalid who suffered from tuberculosis. After she died in 1847, Poe became very depressed, and his last years were grim. Many critics blamed his problems on his heavy drinking.

In 1849 Poe became engaged to a woman he had known since childhood. A short time before the wedding date, however, he was found lying on a street in Baltimore in a coma. He died without regaining consciousness. Poe was only forty years old.

Although Poe wrote both stories and poetry, he is probably best known today as the author of horror stories such as "The Tell-Tale Heart," "The Pit and the Pendulum," and "The Fall of the House of Usher." He is also credited with the early development of two other types of stories—the detective story and science fiction. Today an award called the "Edgar," in Poe's honor, is given each year to the author of the best mystery story.

Edna St. Vincent Millay, author of "Recuerdo," was born in Rockland, Maine in 1892. As a child, she began writing poetry and pursuing her interest in music and theater. In high school she edited and wrote poems for the school magazine.

In 1917, after graduating from Vassar College and publishing her first book of poetry, Millay moved to Greenwich Village in New York City. There she continued to publish poetry and she also wrote, directed, and acted in plays. Millay enjoyed giving poetry readings. One listener described her as "unusually beautiful, sustained in any mood by her bright and lively hair. . . . Saying her poems aloud on a stage, she became tall with her friendly dignity. Her voice was extraordinary."

In 1923 Millay won a Pulitzer Prize for her volume *The Harp-Weaver and Other Poems.* That same year she married and moved to a farm in upstate New York. She continued to write poems until her death in 1950. Today Millay's poems are admired for their technical excellence and their joyful approach to life.

Lesson Preview

The lesson that follows the two poems in this chapter focuses on those elements that give poetry its unique sound. You will examine four elements of sound—repetition, rhyme, rhythm, and meter—and learn how they work individually and together to create a poem's musical quality.

The best way to approach a poem for the first time is to read it all the way through without stopping. Listen to its sounds. Notice the punctuation and the pauses, and listen for the repetition of sounds and the rhymes. Reread the poem several more times. Notice how the poet uses sound to emphasize certain words or phrases.

The questions that follow will help you listen to the poems by Poe and Millay. As you read, think about how you would answer these questions.

1 What kinds of repetition occur in "Annabel Lee"?

2 Which lines are repeated in "Recuerdo"? What other kinds of repetition do you notice?

3 Do any words or lines rhyme in "Annabel Lee" or in "Recuerdo"? Where do the rhymes occur?

4 What other patterns of sound do you notice in the two poems?

Vocabulary

Here are some difficult words that appear in the poems that follow. Study the words and their definitions, as well as the sentences that show how the words are used. This will help you get the most from your reading.

seraphs angels. *The exterior of the cathedral was decorated with many ornate stone seraphs.*

coveted desired enviously. *The hungry child coveted the breads and pastries displayed in the baker's window.*

sepulcher a burial vault; tomb. *Although the inscription on the ancient sepulcher had faded away, the structure itself was still solid.*

dissever come apart; separate. *Tired of quarreling with his roommate, the student decided to dissever their relationship and move out of the apartment.*

wan colorless; pale. *Because the sick woman had been indoors for several months, her skin was pale and wan from lack of sunshine.*

Annabel Lee

Edgar Allan Poe

It was many and many a year ago,
    In a kingdom by the sea,
That a maiden there lived whom you may know
    By the name of ANNABEL LEE;
5 And this maiden she lived with no other thought
    Than to love and be loved by me.

I was a child and *she* was a child,
    In this kingdom by the sea:
But we loved with a love that was more than love—
10   I and my ANNABEL LEE;
With a love that the winged seraphs of heaven
    Coveted her and me.

And this was the reason that, long ago,
    In this kingdom by the sea,
15 A wind blew out of a cloud, chilling
    My beautiful ANNABEL LEE;
So that her high-born kinsman came
    And bore her away from me,
To shut her up in a sepulcher
20   In this kingdom by the sea.

The angels, not half so happy in heaven,
    Went envying her and me—
Yes!—that was the reason (as all men know,
    In this kingdom by the sea)
25 That the wind came out of the cloud by night,
    Chilling and killing my ANNABEL LEE.

But our love it was stronger by far than the love
    Of those who were older than we—
    Of many far wiser than we—
30 And neither the angels in heaven above,
    Nor the demons down under the sea,
Can ever dissever my soul from the soul
    Of the beautiful ANNABEL LEE.

For the moon never beams, without bringing me dreams
35   Of the beautiful ANNABEL LEE;
And the stars never rise, but I feel the bright eyes
    Of the beautiful ANNABEL LEE;
And so, all the night-tide, I lie down by the side
Of my darling—my darling—my life and my bride,
40   In the sepulcher there by the sea,
    In her tomb by the sounding sea.

Recuerdo

EDNA ST. VINCENT MILLAY

We were very tired, we were very merry—
We had gone back and forth all night on the ferry.
It was bare and bright, and smelled like a stable—
But we looked into a fire, we leaned across a table,
5 We lay on a hill-top underneath the moon;
And the whistles kept blowing, and the dawn came soon.

We were very tired, we were very merry—
We had gone back and forth all night on the ferry;
And you ate an apple, and I ate a pear,
10   From a dozen of each we had bought somewhere;
And the sky went wan, and the wind came cold,
And the sun rose dripping, a bucketful of gold.

We were very tired, we were very merry,
We had gone back and forth all night on the ferry.
15   We hailed, "Good morrow, mother!" to a shawl-covered head,
And bought a morning paper, which neither of us read;
And she wept, "God bless you!" for the apples and pears,
And we gave her all our money but our subway fares.

Reviewing the Selections

Answer each of the following questions. You may look back at the poems if necessary.

Recalling Facts

1. "Annabel Lee" takes place
   □ a. in a Scottish castle in the eighteenth century.
   □ b. on a tree-lined street in Baltimore in the 1920s.
   □ c. in a kingdom by the sea long ago.
   □ d. in a mansion in the South during the Civil War.

Understanding Main Ideas

2. What is the most important emotion felt by the speaker in "Annabel Lee"?
   □ a. intense, undying love
   □ b. sincere affection
   □ c. bitter anger
   □ d. peaceful acceptance

Placing Events in Order

3. After Annabel Lee dies, what does the speaker do "all the night-tide"?
   □ a. stares out at the sea
   □ b. weeps quietly at home
   □ c. writes poems in memory of her
   □ d. lies down beside her tomb

Finding Supporting Details

4. In "Recuerdo" the speaker describes the ferry as
   □ a. crowded and noisy.
   □ b. dark, damp, and slippery.
   □ c. bare, bright, and smelling like a stable.
   □ d. clean, dry, and looking like a ship.

5. "We <u>hailed</u>, 'Good morrow, mother!' to a shawl-
covered head." In this context *hailed* means
☐ a. rained on.
☐ b. greeted warmly.
☐ c. threw stones at.
☐ d. sang loudly.

Interpreting the Selections

Answer each of the following questions. You may look back at the poems if
necessary.

6. From the poem, what can you infer about Annabel
Lee's death?
☐ a. A relative murdered her.
☐ b. The speaker caused her to
drown accidentally.
☐ c. Her disease was hereditary.
☐ d. She died suddenly and unexpectedly.

7. Consider the speaker's words and actions in
"Annabel Lee." Which pair of adjectives best
describes his character?
☐ a. intense and brooding
☐ b. serious and philosophical
☐ c. lighthearted and whimsical
☐ d. unforgiving and cold

8. In "Recuerdo" the poet's main purpose is to
   - ☐ a. express compassion for the homeless.
   - ☐ b. recall a moment of sadness.
   - ☐ c. remember a carefree, happy time shared with a loved one.
   - ☐ d. describe how it feels to stay up all night.

Comparing

9. Both "Annabel Lee" and "Recuerdo" tell about
   - ☐ a. a death by drowning.
   - ☐ b. a time of shared love.
   - ☐ c. the sadness of growing old.
   - ☐ d. the joys of childhood.

Drawing
Conclusions

10. In "Recuerdo" which of the following statements best summarizes the speaker's attitude toward life?
    - ☐ a. We should always look to a brighter future.
    - ☐ b. We should live each moment to the fullest.
    - ☐ c. The past is best forgotten.
    - ☐ d. Youth is better than old age.

Sound in Poetry

Just as songs are meant to be sung, poetry is written to be heard. In order to hear a poem, you must listen to its sounds. Even though you may be reading a poem silently, you can still learn to listen to it.

In this lesson you will study the sounds in two poems: "Annabel Lee" and "Recuerdo." Both Poe and Millay have chosen words and sounds to emphasize the emotions they describe in their poems.

Repetition

When you read a poem for the first time, listen for an overall pattern of sound. In some poems you will hear certain sounds, words, or phrases repeated. In poetry repetition is the reappearance of a sound, a word, a phrase, or a line.

Poets use repetition for several reasons. They may want to emphasize an idea or intensify an emotion, or they might want to create tension, express excitement, or convey relief. A person might say, for example, "I want to leave immediately. Immediately!" The repetition of *immediately* emphasizes the wish, clarifies the emotion, and makes you feel the speaker's excitement.

In "Annabel Lee" the speaker, the voice that talks in a poem, repeats the name of his beloved. The repetition of Annabel Lee's name reinforces the speaker's feelings of love and devotion. Notice, too, that she is often referred to as the "beautiful Annabel Lee," emphasizing her physical appearance.

1. In addition to the repetition of the name, what line is repeated throughout "Annabel Lee"? What idea or feeling does that repetition suggest?

Refrain

Repetition is a musical device that is frequently used in songs and poems. Many familiar songs regularly repeat certain lines. Think of two songs you probably learned as a child: "Three Blind Mice" and "The Farmer in the Dell." Both contain a kind of repetition called a refrain—one or more lines that are repeated throughout a song or poem.

In poetry a refrain usually appears at the beginning or the end of a stanza. A stanza is a group of lines that forms a section of the poem. Like other kinds of repetition, a refrain adds a musical quality and emphasizes an idea or an emotion.

2. Reread the three stanzas in "Recuerdo." What is the poem's refrain? Where does it occur? What does it emphasize in the poem?

Rhyme

Another form of repetition in poetry is rhyme. Rhyme is the repetition of the same or similar sound or sounds. Rhyme is often related to meaning because it brings two or more words together. *Lean/clean, clog/fog,* and *grumbling/tumbling* are examples of rhyming words.

Poetry contains various kinds of rhyme. Some rhymes are classified according to their position in a poem. One kind of rhyme that depends on position is end rhyme—the repetition of syllable sounds that occurs at the ends of lines. The following lines from "Recuerdo" are an example of end rhyme:

> It was bare and bright, and smelled like a *stable*—
> But we looked into a fire, we leaned across a *table,*

Another kind of rhyme that depends on position is internal rhyme—rhyme that occurs when a word within a line rhymes with another word in the line. Notice how Poe uses internal rhyme in this line: "For the moon never *beams,* without bringing me *dreams.*" The rhyming of *beams* and *dreams* focuses attention on both words.

3. Reread both poems and find two other examples of end rhyme and internal rhyme.

Some rhymes depend on their stress instead of their position in the poem. Stress refers to words or syllables that receive greater accent, or emphasis, than others. Stress gives a word or syllable greater force or prominence in a line of poetry.

Two types of rhyme that depend on stressed syllables are feminine and masculine rhyme. Rhymes that consist of a stressed syllable followed by one or two unstressed syllables *(chilling, killing)* are called feminine rhymes. Rhymes of one stressed syllable *(sea, Lee)* are called masculine rhymes. Masculine and feminine rhymes can be positioned as either end rhymes or internal rhymes.

Feminine rhyme adds a lightness and grace to poetry, especially when it is used with the sharp, strong sounds of masculine rhyme. Poets use the contrast between feminine and masculine rhyme not only to enrich the mood but also to contribute to the meaning of the words in the poem.

4. Reread "Recuerdo." Find one example of masculine rhyme and one example of feminine rhyme.

Why Poets Use Rhyme

Rhyme, like repetition, is important in poetry because it gives a musical quality to a poem. Like refrains, rhymes can produce a sense of expectation. Once you discover that the poem has a rhyme pattern, you expect that rhyming sound to recur.

Rhyme helps to unify a poem by emphasizing the relationships between lines. Thoughts, feelings, and ideas can be linked through rhyme. In addition, a poet's use of rhyme can contribute to the mood, or the general feeling or atmosphere created in a poem, as well as to the meaning.

In lines 11 and 12 of "Recuerdo," for example, the speaker describes the changes in light and temperature at sunrise. The poet connects the lines with an end rhyme:

And the sky went wan, and the wind came cold,
And the sun rose dripping, a bucketful of gold.

The sun's gold contrasts with the wind's cold, and the end rhyme links the two images. An <u>image</u> is a word or phrase that creates a mental picture of something for the reader. Images are often visual, but they can also appeal to sensations of sound, taste, smell, and touch. By using rhyme to connect those two images in the poem, Millay draws a vivid picture of the scene.

5. Analyze the end rhymes and the internal rhymes in "Annabel Lee." Are more of them masculine or feminine? What mood do they create?

Rhyme Schemes

In addition to creating a musical quality in a poem, rhyme also builds a structure that can unify a poem. This structure is called the rhyme scheme. <u>Rhyme scheme</u> is the pattern of end rhyme in a poem. A poem has a rhyme scheme when the words at the ends of two or more lines rhyme. You can identify a rhyme scheme by assigning a different letter of the alphabet to each line-end sound in a stanza, beginning with the letter *a*. Lines that rhyme are given the same letter. The rhyme scheme for the opening stanza of "Annabel Lee," for example, is *ababcb*:

It was many and many a year ago,	*a*
In a kingdom by the sea,	*b*
That a maiden there lived whom you may know	*a*
By the name of ANNABEL LEE;	*b*
And this maiden she lived with no other thought	*c*
Than to love and be loved by me.	*b*

When identifying the rhyme scheme of a poem, you assign the same letter throughout the poem to lines that end in the same sound. In "Annabel Lee" the end sound *ee*, as in *sea* and *Lee*, will always be assigned the letter *b*.

6. Identify the rhyme scheme in the other stanzas of "Annabel Lee." Remember to assign a new letter to each new line-end sound. How does the rhyme scheme of the second stanza compare with the first stanza?

7. What is the rhyme scheme of the first stanza of "Recuerdo"?

Why should you analyze the rhyme scheme of a poem? Poets use rhyme to emphasize certain ideas and images or to produce a special sound effect. By analyzing the rhyme scheme of a poem, you not only identify the pattern of sound but you also understand the poet's purpose in using that pattern.

Rhythm

Another important sound pattern in poetry is rhythm. Rhythm is the pattern of stressed and unstressed syllables in a poem. This pattern produces a beat in poetry, just as it does in music. Like rhythm in music, rhythm in poetry can be rapid or slow, unsettling or calming, mournful or excited. As with other kinds of repetition, rhythm can give a musical quality to a poem and support the meaning or mood of the poem.

8. Quickly reread "Annabel Lee," listening this time for its rhythm. What adjectives would you choose to describe the rhythm of the poem? Does the rhythm suit the sense and the mood of the poem? Explain your answers.

9. How would you describe the rhythm of "Recuerdo"? How does the rhythm contribute to the poem's mood?

Meter

As you have learned, the rhythm of a poem has a pattern of stressed and unstressed syllables. Meter is the regular pattern of stressed and unstressed syllables in a line of poetry. Studying a poem's meter helps you to analyze the rhythm of the poem. If you can recognize the meter, then you can understand how the rhythm is created and how it works in the poem.

Meter is based on the occurrence of stressed and unstressed syllables in words. In the word *beautiful,* for example, the first syllable is stressed, while the second and third syllables are unstressed. You say the word as BEAU-ti-ful. Poets control the meter of their poems by carefully analyzing the words in lines. To analyze the rhythmic pattern, or meter, of a line of poetry, you indicate the stressed and unstressed syllables with these signs: / for a stressed syllable and ‿ for an unstressed syllable. You would mark the stress pattern of the word *beautiful* as beáutiful. The process of counting the number and arrangement of stressed and unstressed syllables in a line is called <u>scanning</u>.

10. Write down the following phrases: Annabel Lee, the sounding sea, the wind came cold, bucketful of gold. *Scan for stressed and unstressed syllables and mark the stress pattern of each phrase.*

Meter is measured in units called feet. A <u>foot</u> consists of one stressed syllable and its one or more unstressed syllables. There are many kinds of feet in English verse. The most common poetic feet are:

iamb one unstressed syllable followed one stressed syllable: a gó

trochee one stressed syllable followed by one unstressed syllable: kíng dom

anapest two unstressed syllables followed by one stressed syllable: un der neáth

dactyl one stressed syllable followed by two unstressed syllables: beáu ti ful

spondee two stressed syllables: á mén

The meter of a line of poetry refers to the kind of foot and to the number of feet in the line. The following terms refer to the number of feet: trimeter (three feet), tetrameter (four feet), pentameter (five feet), hexameter (six feet). Thus, a line of verse containing four anapests is called *anapestic tetrameter.* "Annabel Lee" contains examples of anapestic tetrameter:

But our lóve   it was stróng   er by fár   than the lóve

1   2   3   4

<u>Iambic pentameter</u> is the most frequently used line of verse in English poetry. It consists of a five-foot line in which each foot is an iamb. When you are analyzing the meter of a poem, you may notice that the pattern is not always regular in every line. If that is the case, decide what meter a line *nearly* matches.

11. Choose one line from each of the poems in this chapter. Indicate the stressed and unstressed syllables and divide the lines into feet. Identify the type of foot and the number of feet in each line. Then name the meter.

Poets often vary the meter to force you to read in a certain way. The meter, for example, may cause you to slow down or speed up in certain sections of the poem.

Reread "Annabel Lee," exaggerating the stressed syllables. Notice how Poe focuses your attention on certain ideas, thoughts, and feelings. In the first stanza, for example, he emphasizes the words *many, kingdom, maiden, name, Annabel Lee, thought,* and *love.* The stressed words highlight the major ideas that Poe returns to later in the poem.

12. *Look at the last stanza of "Annabel Lee." What words receive the strongest stress? What ideas or feelings do those words convey?*

Repetition, rhyme, rhythm, and meter are some of the elements of sound that influence what you hear when you read a poem. Those elements of sound help you to understand the meaning and mood of a poem.

Questions for Thought and Discussion

The questions and activities that follow will help you explore the poems in this chapter in more depth and at the same time develop your critical thinking skills.

1. **Analyzing Character.** The speaker in a poem is like the narrator in a story. Reread "Recuerdo." What impression do you have of the speaker's character in "Recuerdo"? How is the speaker in that poem different from the speaker in "Annabel Lee"?

2. **Comparing Moods.** The moods of "Annabel Lee" and "Recuerdo" are very different. What words would you use to describe the mood in each? What details—words, images, actions—help create the mood in each poem?

3. **Evaluating What You Hear.** Divide the class into small groups. Each group should choose one of the poems to recite aloud. Begin by discussing the repetition, rhyme, rhythm, and meter in each stanza of the poem. Decide

how those elements can be used to help listeners understand the poem. Then assign each stanza to a different student in the group. Each student should practice saying the stanza aloud, trying to recite it as the group has decided the poet intended it to sound. Volunteers from each group can recite the poems to the class.

Writing About Literature

Several suggestions for writing projects are given below. You may be asked to complete one or more of these projects. If you have any questions about how to begin a writing assignment, review Using the Writing Process, beginning on page 219.

1. **Explaining a Choice.** Imagine that you could spend some time with the speaker in one of the poems you read. In a paragraph or two, explain which speaker you would choose. Give reasons for your choice.

2. **Analyzing Rhythm.** Choose one of the poems and write several paragraphs analyzing its rhythm. First identify the general meter. Then describe the effect of the rhythm. Suggest how the rhythm reinforces the poem's meaning.

3. **Writing a Detailed Description.** Think of a scene, an event, or an activity that happened to you in a very brief period of time. It might be entering school for the first time, riding a chair lift, falling off a skateboard, or any other topic. If you prefer, you can simply invent a scene. In either case, think of the general feeling, or mood, of the scene. Focus on as many details as you can about the scene: What did you see, hear, smell, taste, or touch? How, precisely, did you feel? What exactly did you do? After reliving the scene, write a detailed description in which you communicate what you felt at the time.

Chapter 2

Selection *Fern Hill*

DYLAN THOMAS

Lesson *Sound and Meaning*

About the Selection

Think about what a wonderful part memory plays in your life. Your memory holds all the important experiences, feelings, and impressions that are vital parts of your life. Memory keeps the door open to your past.

In order to appreciate the importance that memory plays in your life, imagine how limited your life would be without it. Experiences would have no lasting effect. You would not learn from your mistakes or your accomplishments. Because time would have no meaning, you would not recollect your childhood or remember growing up. You would exist only from moment to moment. Clearly, memory is necessary in order to achieve even simple goals.

"Fern Hill" by Dylan Thomas is a poem about memory. The speaker recalls a variety of incidents and impressions from his childhood—the sights and sounds of nature, the joy of physical activity, the absence of care. However, the poem is also about the way memory works. When you remember an experience or a certain time in your life, a number of impressions often overlap. Instead of remembering separate events or feelings, you recall several feelings at the same time.

In "Fern Hill" Dylan Thomas creates a pattern of continuously changing, complex feelings. Some lines of the poem are long and are filled with details while other lines are short. The poet creates unusual images by combining words and phrases in unexpected ways. Remind yourself, however, that the subject of the poem is memory. Instead of describing events and actions as they actually happened, Thomas has recollections slide together. He not only recalls childhood but also helps you understand how memory works.

Despite the complexity of his writing, Dylan Thomas is one of the most respected poets of the twentieth century. Readers have praised his humor, the beauty of his language, and the richness of his images, as well as his passionate interest in life and living things.

Dylan Thomas was born in 1914 in Swansea, Wales, and spent his childhood there. He often visited his aunt's farm in Llangain, where he immersed himself in nature and in literature. Those childhood visits to Llangain provided the setting for "Fern Hill."

At the age of twenty, Thomas published his first book, *Eighteen Poems*, and the praise it received encouraged him to continue publishing his poems. During World War II he moved to London where he served as an antiaircraft gunner and wrote film and radio scripts for the British Broadcasting Company (BBC). In the early 1950s Thomas made several successful tours of the United States. He was an impressive reader of poetry, and his fine voice attracted large audiences to his poetry readings.

In addition to poetry, Dylan Thomas wrote short stories and essays, as well as a voice play called *Under Milk Wood.* His reminiscences, *A Child's Christmas in Wales,* are still very popular. Dylan Thomas died of pneumonia in 1953, while on tour in New York City.

Lesson Preview

In Chapter 1 you learned how repetition, rhyme, rhythm, and meter contribute to the musical quality of poetry. The lesson that follows "Fern Hill" focuses on other ways in which poets use sound. Because the sounds of words can suggest certain feelings or images, poets often choose a particular word for its sound to add meaning to their poems.

As you read "Fern Hill," notice how Dylan Thomas uses sound in the poem to support its meaning. The questions that follow will help you identify the sounds of the poem. As you read, think about how you would answer these questions.

1 Notice repetition in the poem. What phrases, images, and sounds are repeated? What purpose do you think those repetitions serve?

2 Do the sounds of any words or phrases seem unusual?

3 What feelings are expressed in "Fern Hill"?

4 What kinds of actions are described? What kinds of details does the speaker give you?

5 What do you think the poet is saying about time? Do you agree with his opinion?

Vocabulary

Here are some difficult words that appear in the poem that follows. Study the words and their definitions, as well as the sentences that show how the words are used. This will help you get the most from your reading.

lilting cheerful; buoyant. *A robin's lilting song is often the first sign that winter is over.*

windfall something blown down by the wind. *The gusting winds left us with a windfall of ripe, red apples.*

heedless careless; thoughtless. *The gambler, always heedless about money, continued to lose bets at the horse races.*

thronged crowded. *The theater was so thronged with people that it was almost impossible to find a seat.*

Fern Hill

Dylan Thomas

Now as I was young and easy under the apple boughs
About the lilting house and happy as the grass was green,
    The night above the dingle[1] starry,
      Time let me hail and climb
5   Golden in the heydays[2] of his eyes,
And honored among wagons I was prince of the apple towns
And once below a time I lordly had the trees and leaves
      Trail with daisies and barley
    Down the rivers of the windfall light.

10   And as I was green and carefree, famous among the barns
About the happy yard and singing as the farm was home,
    In the sun that is young once only,
      Time let me play and be
    Golden in the mercy of his means,
15 And green and golden I was huntsman and herdsman, the calves
Sang to my horn, the foxes on the hills barked clear and cold,
      And the sabbath[3] rang slowly
    In the pebbles of the holy streams.

All the sun long it was running, it was lovely, the hay
20 Fields high as the house, the tunes from the chimneys, it was air
      And playing, lovely and watery
      And fire green as grass.

---

1. dingle: small, deep, wooded valley.   **2. heydays:** times of greatest success or strength.   **3. sabbath:** the first day of the week, Sunday, set aside for rest and worship by Christians.

And nightly under the simple stars
As I rode to sleep the owls were bearing the farm away,
25   All the moon long I heard, blessed among stables, the nightjars[4]
      Flying with the ricks,[5] and the horses
        Flashing into the dark.

And then to awake, and the farm, like a wanderer white
With the dew, come back, the cock on his shoulder: it was all
30   Shining, it was Adam and maiden,
         The sky gathered again
      And the sun grew round that very day.
So it must have been after the birth of the simple light
In the first, spinning place, the spellbound horses walking warm
35   Out of the whinnying green stable
        On to the fields of praise.

And honored among foxes and pheasants by the gay house
Under the new made clouds and happy as the heart was long,
      In the sun born over and over,
40   I ran my heedless ways,
      My wishes raced through the house high hay
And nothing I cared, at my sky blue trades, that time allows
In all his tuneful turning so few and such morning songs
      Before the children green and golden
45   Follow him out of grace,

---

4. nightjars: night birds that sing. **5. ricks:** haystacks.

Nothing I cared, in the lamb white days, that time would take me
Up to the swallow thronged loft by the shadow of my hand,
   In the moon that is always rising,
    Nor that riding to sleep
50   I should hear him fly with the high fields
And wake to the farm forever fled from the childless land.
Oh as I was young and easy in the mercy of his means,
    Time held me green and dying
   Though I sang in my chains like the sea.

Reviewing the Selection

Answer each of the following questions. You may look back at the poem if necessary.

Recalling Facts

1. The poem takes place in
   - ☐ a. winter in the country.
   - ☐ b. autumn near a city park.
   - ☐ c. springtime on a lake.
   - ☐ d. summer on a farm.

Understanding Main Ideas

2. Which of the following statements best expresses the main idea of the poem?
   - ☐ a. We should love and protect our children because childhood is full of sorrow and pain.
   - ☐ b. Spare the rod and spoil the child.
   - ☐ c. For all its freedom and joy, childhood is part of a progression toward death.
   - ☐ d. The joys of adults are nothing compared to those of children.

Placing Events in Order

3. When did the speaker recognize that time does not allow anything in life to last for long?
   - ☐ a. when he was grown
   - ☐ b. when he was a child on the farm
   - ☐ c. in the early morning
   - ☐ d. while playing in the fields

Finding Supporting Details

4. Thomas uses colors to suggest both the season and his feelings. The most important colors in "Fern Hill" are
   - ☐ a. blue and brown.
   - ☐ b. orange and red.
   - ☐ c. green and gold.
   - ☐ d. white and gray.

Sound and Meaning

5. "And once below a time I <u>lordly had</u> the trees and leaves / Trail with daisies and barley." In this context *I lordly had* means I
   - ☐ a. knew.
   - ☐ b. controlled.
   - ☐ c. read.
   - ☐ d. destroyed.

Interpreting the Selection

Answer each of the following questions. You may look back at the poem if necessary.

Making
Inferences

6. Which of the following adjectives best describes how the speaker feels about his childhood?
   - ☐ a. angry and resentful
   - ☐ b. detached
   - ☐ c. cynical
   - ☐ d. grateful and contented

Analyzing
the Evidence

7. The child in the poem is
   - ☐ a. carefree and full of vitality.
   - ☐ b. burdened with many chores.
   - ☐ c. looking forward to becoming an adult.
   - ☐ d. very quiet and shy.

Finding the
Author's Purpose

8. In line 30 the poet refers to Adam because
   - ☐ a. Adam is a common name for an animal.
   - ☐ b. the speaker's name is Adam.
   - ☐ c. the dawn was like the Biblical beginning.
   - ☐ d. Adam also loved the country.

9. The last stanza differs from the rest of the poem because it
   - ☐ a. refers to nighttime and sleep.
   - ☐ b. suggests that the carefree feeling of childhood is an illusion.
   - ☐ c. is twice as long as each of the other stanzas.
   - ☐ d. reminds you that adults can experience as much joy as children.

10. Although "Fern Hill" is primarily about memories, it is also about
    - ☐ a. time.
    - ☐ b. courage.
    - ☐ c. love.
    - ☐ d. loneliness.

Sound and Meaning

Works of art have two main elements: content and form. The content of a story, a film, or a painting is the central idea or feeling it expresses. The form is the way in which the idea is presented and explored.

For example, during one scene in the famous musical *Singin' in the Rain*, a man realizes that he is in love. To express his joy, he dances in the street, even though the rain is pouring down. The central idea of the scene is simple: the man is in love. The idea is given form in an exuberant dance, full of skipping, spinning, and splashing.

Content and form also coexist in poetry. An important aspect of poetic form is sound, and a poem's sound and content are interconnected. In this lesson you will study how sound and meaning are combined in "Fern Hill."

Understanding the Poem

"Fern Hill" is about memory. The speaker in the poem is recollecting his childhood. Throughout the poem, you observe the child's activities, and you hear his observations about the world around him.

You feel that the child is enjoying life and is not very aware of time passing. Yet the speaker is aware of the passage of time. He reflects on the pleasures he experienced in the sunny summer days when he was young. The poet shows you how the mind selects details and compresses events, and how memories are a part of impressions and images.

1. In stanza 1 what actions or incidents does the speaker describe?

2. What emotions are felt by the speaker? What emotions are felt by the child? How does the poet express those feelings?

The four middle stanzas in "Fern Hill" re-create the experiences and feelings of the child's carefree summer days. The boy plays on the farm, imagines himself as "huntsman and herdsman," enjoys the sounds of the animals, and "runs his heedless ways."

In the last stanza, however, the poem changes. Earlier in the poem, time was friendly to the carefree child. But at the end of the poem, time is less kind and more threatening.

> Time held me green and dying
> Though I sang in my chains like the sea.

The speaker suggests that in the midst of the joys of childhood something more serious is happening. Time holds the boy "green and dying," suggesting that even when he was young, he was moving toward death. The boy, unaware of any threat, says, "I sang in my chains like the sea." Now an older and wiser man, the speaker understands the bonds in which time held him.

Mood and Atmosphere

In "Fern Hill" Dylan Thomas is less interested in describing specific actions and events than in creating impressions. He re-creates his childhood by recalling its mood, or general feeling or atmosphere. Thomas recalls the mood by selecting and arranging details to create a series of images. The images he draws suggest a childhood brimming with happiness and adventure. In stanza 1, for example, the speaker says:

> And once below a time I lordly had the trees and leaves
> Trail with daisies and barley
> Down the rivers of the windfall light.

Notice that the images and details blend together, making it difficult to select individual images. Trees and leaves flow into daisies and barley. Everything seems to float together along rivers of falling light. The child "lordly" reigns over his kingdom.

3. What mood do the preceding lines create? What specific details help establish that mood?

4. Read lines 19 to 22 in stanza 3. What mood do they create? Is the mood similar to or different from that of stanza 1?

The Role of Sound

In "Fern Hill" Thomas uses sounds to support and deepen the enchantment of the boy's childhood. Thomas uses sounds in different ways and for different purposes. First, the poet chooses words for their musical qualities. Second, he combines words in unusual ways to extend their meanings. Third, he repeats phrases, sometimes with slight changes. Finally, he chooses certain vowel and consonant sounds to create specific patterns and effects. All these devices contribute to the nostalgic, romantic mood of the poem.

Diction. All good writers select their words carefully. Poets, because they compress many ideas and feelings into a few words, must take special care to choose words that express precisely what they mean. A poet's choice and arrangement of words is called diction.

Dylan Thomas chose many of the words in "Fern Hill" for their musical qualities. Read the first stanza aloud and listen to the sound of each word. Certain words, you may notice, stand out because of their sounds.

5. List the words in stanza 1 that you think have a musical quality.

Thomas chooses specific words and then carefully combines them to add meaning to the poem. "Fern Hill" uses unusual and playful word combinations: "About the lilting house," "honored among wagons," "famous among the barns," "All the sun long it was running," "the lamb white days."

Such phrases do not make literal sense. What is a "lilting house"? What does the poet mean by "All the sun long it was running"? Both phrases, however, suggest certain images. The word *lilting* means singing or playing with a light, graceful rhythm. Combined with the word *house*, it suggests that even the walls of the child's home echoed with happy sounds. "All the sun long" is an unusual way of saying "all day long." And "it was running" might refer to the child's constant activity and movement.

Phrases such as those are puzzling at first, and they make you work harder to understand the poem. Yet they give you a new way of viewing the idea, feeling, or thought that Thomas describes.

6. Choose two other unusual phrases in the poem. Explain what you think each means. How does the sound of each phrase contribute to its meaning?

Repetition. In Chapter 1 you learned how repetition adds to the musical quality of a poem. In "Fern Hill" you can identify several examples of repetition. The phrase "green and golden" appears in lines 15 and 44. That phrase creates an image of youth and abundance—the green growth of plants in the summer and the golden sunshine that nourishes them.

The phrase "All the sun long" (line 19) recurs as "All the moon long" in line 25. Both phrases suggest an endless stretch of time.

7. Find two other repetitions of phrases. Explain what idea each suggests.

Alliteration and Assonance

In "Fern Hill" Thomas uses other devices of sound that create a musical pattern and support the mood of the poem. One such device is alliteration—the close repetition of the same first sounds in words, usually consonant sounds. You often hear alliteration in everyday phrases as well as in advertising slogans. Thomas's poem has many examples of alliteration. Read line 2:

About the lilting house and happy as the grass was green,

The same alliteration occurs in reverse order in line 15:

And green and golden I was huntsman and herdsman . . .

The use of alliteration in those lines emphasizes the words that share the same first sounds. It also adds to the musical quality of the lines.

8. Identify at least three other examples of alliteration in "Fern Hill." Choose one of those examples and explain how it affects the poem.

Another device of sound that Thomas uses is <u>assonance</u>—the repetition of similar vowel sounds within words. As with other devices of sound, assonance focuses attention on certain sounds and adds a musical quality. Read line 10 aloud and listen to the repetition of the *a* sounds. Although the *a* sounds are not identical, they are similar.

<u>A</u>nd <u>a</u>s I w<u>a</u>s green <u>a</u>nd c<u>a</u>refree, f<u>a</u>mous <u>a</u>mong the b<u>a</u>rns

In that line the repetition of the *a* sound connects the images of a happy, busy child.

9. Read line 47. What vowel sounds are repeated? What effect does assonance have on the meaning of that line?

Assonance and alliteration enhance the mood of the poem and help express its meaning. In the examples you have studied, the repeated consonants are "soft" sounds—*g* and *h*. Similarly, the long vowel sounds—*o* and *a*—also add softness to the poem. The use of soft consonants and long vowels gives a quiet, whispered quality to "Fern Hill." When you read the poem aloud, you can hear how words and phrases are lengthened, or extended, by those soft sounds.

Questions for Thought and Discussion

The questions and activities that follow will help you explore "Fern Hill" in more depth and at the same time develop your critical thinking skills.

1. **Analyzing the Mood.** List several adjectives that describe the mood of "Fern Hill." Then explain what elements Dylan Thomas uses to create the mood. Think about his choice of words and details as well as the colors, images, effects of sound, and rhythm of the poem.

2. **Organizing a Group Reading.** Divide the class into six groups. Each group should prepare one stanza of "Fern Hill" to present as a reading. In your group discuss the meaning of your stanza, as well as the rhythm and

movement of each line. Decide where to pause and what words or phrases to emphasize. You might take turns reading individual lines or choose to read some lines in unison. Try reading lines at different speeds. Finally, have someone from each group read a stanza, presenting the stanzas in their proper order.

3. **Interpreting Details.** Think about the colors in the poem. Which colors dominate? What thoughts, feelings, or ideas do those colors suggest? What do the colors represent in the poem? What colors do you associate with your childhood? Explain your answer.

Writing About Literature

Several suggestions for writing projects are given below. You may be asked to complete one or more of these projects. If you have any questions about how to begin a writing assignment, review Using the Writing Process, beginning on page 219.

1. **Comparing.** You have already identified some differences between the last stanza in "Fern Hill" and the rest of the poem. Compare the poet's attitude toward childhood in the last stanza to the attitude expressed in the rest of the poem. Why do you think Thomas introduced this new idea in the last stanza?

2. **Writing About Sound in Poetry.** Review what you learned in Chapters 1 and 2 about the various ways in which poets use sound. Then reread "Fern Hill." Choose one stanza in "Fern Hill" and analyze its elements of sound. Write one or two paragraphs explaining how those elements contribute to the meaning of the poem.

3. **Describing a Childhood Experience.** Recall an experience from your own childhood. Using poetry or prose, describe that experience. Your description should let readers understand the incident and what details or images remain strong in your mind. Write about your experience as Dylan Thomas did, recalling impressions and images as well as the mood of the experience.

Chapter 3

Selections

Pied Beauty

GERARD MANLEY HOPKINS

may my heart always be open to little

E. E. CUMMINGS

Susie Asado

GERTRUDE STEIN

Lesson

The Sounds of Words

About the Selections

A poet's creativity depends to a great extent on his or her freedom to experiment with language. Through experimentation, a poet may develop variations on familiar themes and techniques or perhaps invent a completely new way in which to express ideas.

Every age has had poets who have rejected the traditional approach to poetry. They have broken rules about proper subject matter, structure, and elements of sound. Some poets have experimented with style, such as line length, word arrangement, meter, rhythm, and even the physical appearance of words on the page.

The authors of the three poems in this chapter are among the most innovative poets of their eras. Gerard Manley Hopkins, the author of "Pied Beauty," was born in Essex, England, in 1844. While he was a student at Oxford University, he experienced a spiritual crisis that led him to become a Roman Catholic. In 1868, at the age of twenty-two, Hopkins entered the Society of Jesus, better known as the Jesuit religious order.

Hopkins taught at Catholic schools in England and Scotland before being appointed professor of Greek at University College in Dublin, Ireland. He held that position until his death in 1889.

Hopkins wrote poems throughout most of his life, but never seriously tried to publish his work. At one point in his life, he stopped writing and burned most of his poems. He did eventually resume writing, and his work was published by a friend in 1918. These surviving poems are notable for their unique rhythmic patterns and for Hopkins's experimentation with original word combinations.

E. E. (Edward Estlin) Cummings, who wrote "may my heart always be open to little," was born in Cambridge, Massachusetts, in 1894. After graduating from Harvard College, Cummings joined the American Red Cross and served as an ambulance driver in World War I. By error, the French jailed him for several months on suspicion of treason. His experiences are powerfully recounted in his first book, a novel called *The Enormous Room*.

During the early 1920s, Cummings lived in Paris. In 1923 he returned to the United States and settled in Greenwich Village, a haven for young artists. Cummings was both a poet and a painter, although he is best remembered for his poetry.

Cummings experimented with many physical aspects of poetry. He used typography—the actual printed words and letters—to create word pictures on a page. He stopped using standard capitalization and punctuation and dropped the capital letters from his own name to become e. e. cummings. He put punctuation marks in odd places or capitalized letters in the middle of words in order to draw attention to those words or ideas.

Gertrude Stein (1874–1946) is the author of "Susie Asado," the third poem in this chapter. Although she was born in Allegheny, Pennsylvania, she moved to Paris in the early 1900s and became a leading figure among the experimental artists of that time. Stein's Paris apartment was a gathering place for writers such as Ernest Hemingway and painters such as Henri Matisse and Pablo Picasso. Through her powerful personality, ideas, criticism, and encouragement, Stein influenced many young artists and writers.

Stein's own writing was eccentric, radical, and humorous. She frequently used repetition to communicate ideas; one of her most famous lines is "Rose is a rose is a rose is a rose." In addition to writing poetry, she wrote stories and gave lectures on music, literature, and art. Among her best-known prose works is *The Autobiography of Alice B. Toklas*. In it she draws a portrait of herself as seen through the eyes of Toklas, her friend and secretary.

Lesson Preview

The lesson that follows the poems in this chapter examines how poets experiment with language, and how they use words to enhance the meanings of their poems and to create new meanings and images.

Read each poem at least twice and notice how words and sounds are used. Remember that not all poets intend their poems to make logical sense; meanings often emerge from the way the words sound.

The questions that follow will help you understand how the three poets in this chapter use the sounds of words to create new and unusual meanings. As you read, think about how you would answer these questions.

1 In "Pied Beauty" what is unusual about the poet's choice of words? How does the speaker feel about what he or she sees?

2 What do you notice about the poet's language in "may my heart always be open to little"? What advice is the speaker offering?

3 What sounds dominate "Susie Asado"? How does the poet manipulate the sounds of words?

Vocabulary

Here are some difficult words that appear in the poems that follow. Study the words and their definitions, as well as the sentences that show how the words are used. This will help you get the most from your reading.

pied having patches or blotches of two or more colors. *The horse's pied coat had been brushed until its patches of gray, white, and black gleamed.*

dappled marked with spots or patches. *The sunlight filtered through the trees and formed dappled specks of light on the shady grass.*

supple flexible. *After his accident, the gymnast had to carefully exercise to regain his once supple muscle tone.*

unison complete agreement. *The children sang in unison, their voices blending together perfectly.*

The Sounds of Words

Pied Beauty

GERARD MANLEY HOPKINS

Glory be to God for dappled things—
    For skies of couple-color as a brinded cow;
        For rose-moles all in stipple[1] upon trout that swim;
Fresh-firecoal chestnut-falls; finches' wings;
5   Landscape plotted and pieced—fold, fallow, and plough;[2]
    And áll trádes,[3] their gear and tackle and trim.

All things counter, original, spare, strange;
    Whatever is fickle, freckled (who knows how?)
        With swift, slow; sweet, sour; adazzle, dim;
10 He fathers-forth whose beauty is past change:
        Praise him.

---

1. stipple: dots; flecks. **2. fold:** a hollow; small valley; **fallow:** land that is plowed but not seeded; **plough:** land that is plowed and planted. **3. áll trádes:** the accent marks indicate that both words should be given equal emphasis.

may my heart always be open to little

E. E. CUMMINGS

may my heart always be open to little
birds who are the secrets of living
whatever they sing is better than to know
and if men should not hear them men are old

5   may my mind stroll about hungry
and fearless and thirsty and supple
and even if it's sunday may i be wrong
for whenever men are right they are not young

and may myself do nothing usefully
10   and love yourself so more than truly
there's never been quite such a fool who could fail
pulling all the sky over him with one smile

Susie Asado

GERTRUDE STEIN

Sweet sweet sweet sweet sweet tea
 Susie Asado.
Sweet sweet sweet sweet sweet tea
 Susie Asado.
5 Susie Asado which is a told tray[1] sure.
A lean on the shoe this means slips slips hers.
When the ancient light gray is clean it is yellow, it
is a silver seller.
This is a please this is a please there are the saids to
10 jelly. These are the wets these say the sets to leave a
crown to Incy.
Incy is short for incubus.[2]
A pot. A pot is a beginning of a rare bit of trees.
Trees tremble, the old vats are in bobbles, bobbles which
15 shade and shove and render clean, render clean must.
 Drink pups.
Drink pups drink pups lease a sash hold, see it shine
and a bobolink[3] has pins. It shows a nail.
What is a nail. A nail is unison.
20 Sweet sweet sweet sweet sweet tea.

---

1. **tray:** Stein may be playing with the French word *très,* which is pronounced *tray* and means "very."   **2. incubus:** a demon
spirit.   **3. bobolink:** a migratory songbird.

Reviewing the Selections

Answer each of the following questions. You may look back at the poems if necessary.

Recalling Facts

1. In "Pied Beauty" the speaker praises
   □ a. God.
   □ b. fish.
   □ c. all things in nature.
   □ d. farmers.

Understanding Main Ideas

2. In "may my heart always be open to little," the speaker believes that
   □ a. only young people can enjoy life.
   □ b. people should not close their minds to anything.
   □ c. a person should always try to do what is right.
   □ d. most people are foolish.

Placing Events in Order

3. In "may my heart always be open to little," the speaker talks about keeping his mind open and flexible
   □ a. before he mentions the birds.
   □ b. after he talks about the value of a smile.
   □ c. after he says that men who do not hear the birds are old.
   □ d. after he talks about being wrong even on Sunday.

Finding Supporting Details

4. In "Susie Asado" which sound dominates the poem?
   □ a. *s*
   □ b. *b*
   □ c. *nk*
   □ d. *ee*

5. "In áll trádes, their <u>gear</u> and tackle and trim." In this context *gear* means
   - ☐ a. shift.
   - ☐ b. armor.
   - ☐ c. wheel.
   - ☐ d. equipment.

Interpreting the Selections

Answer each of the following questions. You may look back at the poems if necessary.

6. After reading "Susie Asado," which of the following inferences can you make?
   - ☐ a. Susie Asado was someone Gertrude Stein knew well.
   - ☐ b. Susie Asado was a character in a movie.
   - ☐ c. Gertrude Stein thought Susie Asado was a fool.
   - ☐ d. Gertrude Stein liked the sound of the name Susie Asado.

7. In the poem "may my heart always be open to little," the birds are
   - ☐ a. small but significant because they are caretakers of secret knowledge.
   - ☐ b. more intelligent than humans because they sing all the time.
   - ☐ c. fearless and even sing on Sunday.
   - ☐ d. never foolish.

8. By not using punctuation, E. E. Cummings makes
    - ☐ a. his poem easier to read.
    - ☐ b. you stop longer at the end of each line.
    - ☐ c. ideas and thoughts flow into one another.
    - ☐ d. the poem similar to "Pied Beauty."

Comparing

9. A major difference between "Susie Asado" and the other poems in this chapter is that it
    - ☐ a. has nothing to do with its title.
    - ☐ b. uses alliteration and the others do not.
    - ☐ c. draws a number of seemingly unconnected images.
    - ☐ d. creates images in color.

Drawing
Conclusions

10. Which of the following conclusions can you draw from "Pied Beauty"?
    - ☐ a. The poem is meant to be sung as a hymn.
    - ☐ b. Hopkins prefers natural landscapes to those created by people.
    - ☐ c. Many-colored things are the most beautiful.
    - ☐ d. Hopkins wanted to praise the multicolored creations of God.

The Sounds
of Words

In the first two chapters you learned how important sound is in poetry. All writers appreciate the sounds of words, but poets pay particular attention to sounds.

One way in which poets manipulate sound is by choosing words for sound as well as for meaning. Poets often explore the relationship between a word's meaning and its sound, and he or she may include a specific word because its sound contributes to the meaning of the poem. As you learned in Chapter 2, sound and meaning are closely related in poetry, and sound often reinforces meaning. Sometimes, as you will see in this lesson, sound *is* the meaning.

In each of the poems you have just read, the poet has experimented with both the choice and the arrangement of words. The words have been chosen and arranged with particular concern for how the poem will sound.

Because poets choose their words carefully, they are conscious not only of each word's <u>denotation</u>, or dictionary meaning, but also of each word's connotation. <u>Connotation</u> refers to the emotion that a word arouses or the meanings it suggests beyond its dictionary meaning.

A word's connotation can come from the way it has been used over time. For example, the word *house* denotes a place where you live, but the word *home* connotes, or suggests, a warmer, cozier feeling; *coast* denotes the land next to water, but *seashore* suggests the salty smell of the air, the sights and sounds of the water, and the feel of the sand.

A word's connotation also comes from its context, or how the words that come before or after it influence its meaning. Compare the word *morning* in the next two sentences. "Each day has a *morning,* an afternoon, and an evening." "There will be another *morning,* another dawn." In the first sentence *morning* denotes a time of day. In the second sentence *morning* is influenced by the words around it and suggests a new beginning filled with freshness and energy. Often poets will use a particular word because its connotation reinforces the feeling that they are trying to create.

"Pied Beauty": Reading for Meaning

Gerard Manley Hopkins's "Pied Beauty" is a poem of praise and gratitude to God. The speaker thanks God for the fascinating variety of life in the world. The first stanza is primarily devoted to images of a special kind of beauty— the beauty of things that are "pied" or many-colored. The speaker appreciates the loveliness of "dappled" things, of colors that are mixed, of shapes that are odd, and of things in motion.

1. Describe three things the speaker appreciates. What does the speaker appreciate about "trout that swim"?

2. Does the speaker celebrate only things in nature? Explain your answer.

Diction and Word Combinations

Anyone can list the beautiful things in nature. Part of what makes "Pied Beauty" remarkable is its diction. As you learned in Chapter 2, diction is a poet's choice and arrangement of words. Because poets communicate with very few words, they are especially concerned with the effects of their word choices. In poetry, therefore, individual words and the ways in which they are arranged can be extremely important.

A poet's diction depends on his or her subject, audience, and goals. A poet might choose to use the formal language of scholars and officials, the informal language of everyday speech, or even the slang shared by a particular group. In "Pied Beauty" Hopkins uses archaic, or old-fashioned, language. Notice the words *brinded*, *stipple*, and *adazzle*. *Brinded* is an archaic form of the word *brindled*, which means spotted or streaked with dark color. *Stipple* and *adazzle* were unusual words even in the late 1800s, when Hopkins wrote this poem.

Another feature of Hopkins's diction is his use of unusual word combinations. He combines words in ways that change their literal meanings, suggesting new ideas and creating vivid images. Sometimes the word combinations are as puzzling as they are unusual. In line 4, for example, the exact meaning of "Fresh-firecoal chestnut-falls" is unclear. The two hyphenated words imply a rain of chestnuts pouring to the ground in autumn, just as coals might be poured into a stove to keep the fire burning. Yet other interpretations are possible.

3. Examine the hyphenated word "couple-color" in line 2. What does each word mean separately? What do the joined words suggest?

Hopkins's word combinations build a sense of excitement in the poem. The speaker is recalling all the extraordinary dappled things in the world, and eagerly expressing his observations about them. That eagerness is captured in the way the words are combined. The result is an emotional poem in which the speaker is breathless with enthusiasm. As you read the poem, you may feel breathless, too. Notice how the poem is crowded with words; sometimes almost too many words, as in line 9; "With swift, slow; sweet, sour; adazzle, dim."

4. Find other lines in which the poet has crowded many words together. Read the lines several times. Then reread the entire poem. What effect does the crowding have on the poem?

Experimenting with Language

As you have read, E. E. Cummings used language in unconventional ways. He freed himself from traditional rules of grammar, capitalization, and punctuation. He also invented words, started lines in midsentence, and left lines unfinished. Cummings often used adverbs as adjectives and turned adjectives and verbs into nouns. He would eliminate capital letters and punctuation or use them in unexpected ways. His experimentation forced readers to think more about the relationship between words and meaning.

"may my heart always be open to little" demonstrates some of Cummings's experimentation with language. The poem's speaker suggests several ways to approach living. An awareness of what is simple and beautiful in the world, the speaker says, is one way to remain free-spirited and young. Curiosity, skepticism, open-mindedness, and a willingness to be wrong are essential to living fully.

When you examine the poem, you will notice that the poet uses language in unexpected ways. In line 3, for example, the poet chooses to combine the words in an unusual order: "whatever they sing is better than to know."

5. What is odd about the wording of line 3? What do you think the line means? How does the wording emphasize the meaning?

6. In line 7 which words are not properly capitalized? How do the changes make the words seem different?

Sound as Meaning

The first two poems in the chapter have recognizable meanings and themes. Theme refers to the underlying message of a piece of writing. Gertrude Stein's "Susie Asado" does *not* have a conventional theme. The poem does not tell a story. It does not create a situation or describe a particular feeling, and the words and lines do not make logical sense.

What is "Susie Asado" about? Why was it written? In this extraordinary poem, Gertrude Stein shows you that words can convey meanings beyond the ordinary, logical meanings you expect them to have.

People usually create meaning with language. Language, after all, is how human beings communicate with one another. But how is meaning created? Though every word has a meaning, many words have more than one meaning. And some words may have the same or similar meanings. A word having practically the same meaning as another word is called a synonym. Closely related to a synonym is a homonym—a word that is pronounced like another word but has a different spelling and meaning. *Car* and *auto* are examples of synonyms. Both words have essentially the same meaning. *Write* and *right* are homonyms; they sound alike but are spelled differently and have very different meanings.

"Susie Asado" was inspired by a Spanish flamenco dancer named Susie Asado. Perhaps Stein was simply intrigued by Asado's name, or perhaps the poet was interested in an aspect of her appearance or her character. The poem itself gives no clue about Stein's inspiration. The poet has concentrated on combining words and creating musical sounds, not on producing a logical theme.

The first line, "Sweet sweet sweet sweet sweet tea," is immediately repeated in the second line. Listen to the sound of the words. The repetition of *sweet* creates an image of extreme sweetness. The words suggest the aroma and taste of sugary tea and the pleasure a person feels when drinking sweetened tea.

Read line 6: "A lean on the shoe this means slips slips hers." The word *lean* can be used as a verb (to bend, to depend on) or as an adjective (slender, thin), and it has a number of other meanings, depending on its usage. Was Stein manipulating the word *lean* for a purpose? Although you may not know for certain, you can let the sound of the word influence your imagination.

In the same line Stein repeats the word *slips*. Consider the word's various meanings and listen to its sound. A flamenco dancer might take slipping, sliding steps across the floor, but a dancer can also slip and fall.

Stein enjoys freely associating words and sounds. Free association is a term used by psychologists to mean the process of freely connecting any thoughts or feelings that enter your mind. One thought might lead to a very different thought. In "Susie Asado" Stein explores the sounds and connotations of words, as well as the synonyms and homonyms identified with them.

7. Choose one or two lines from the poem. Reread them several times. Think about how the words sound and what images and feelings they suggest. Describe those images. Do the images suggest anything about what Susie Asado might have been like?

Questions for Thought and Discussion

The questions and activities that follow will help you explore the poems in this chapter in more depth and at the same time develop your critical thinking skills.

1. **Understanding the Author's Purpose.** "Pied Beauty" is a deeply religious poem. Use your own words to explain how the poem reveals the power, grandeur, and "artistry" of God.

2. **Comparing.** Both Hopkins and Cummings focus on appreciating the beauty and variety of the natural world. Although the poems have a similar theme, they move in different directions. Compare and contrast the two poems.

3. **Organizing a Debate.** Organize a debate around the question, Does Gertrude Stein's "Susie Asado" have artistic merit? Each side needs to develop its own criteria for what constitutes artistic merit in a poem. One side should prove that the poem has significant value. The other side should argue that the poem does not have artistic merit.

Writing About Literature

Several suggestions for writing projects are given below. You may be asked to complete one or more of these projects. If you have any questions about how to begin a writing assignment, review Using the Writing Process, beginning on page 219.

1. **Analyzing Diction and Sound.** Choose two poems you studied in this chapter. Reread them, paying particular attention to each poet's choice of words and use of sound. Then compare the two poems, analyzing how the poets use diction and elements of sound to support and deepen the meaning of their poems.

2. **Describing a Quality.** Write a poem or prose description showing how much you admire someone or something. You might begin by noting the qualities of the person or thing that you want to include in your description. Try to write as if you were appreciating the qualities that you are describing for the first time.

3. **Experimenting with Words and Images.** Write a poem or a short prose passage in the manner of "Susie Asado." Decide on a topic. Then think about the feelings you have toward the topic. Choose words and create images that will bring your subject to life for others.

Images
in Poetry

Three Haiku:
*The Chestnut Burr,
Mountain Plum Blossoms,
Lightning at Night*
MATSUO BASHO

The Locust Tree in Flower
WILLIAM CARLOS WILLIAMS

Living
DENISE LEVERTOV

Images and Imagery

I Am Not Yours
SARA TEASDALE

Not Waving but Drowning
STEVIE SMITH

Sonnet 116: Let Me Not to the Marriage of True Minds
WILLIAM SHAKESPEARE

Figurative Language

The Secret Heart
ROBERT P. TRISTRAM COFFIN

The Song of Wandering Aengus
WILLIAM BUTLER YEATS

Imagery, Metaphor, and Symbols

*I*n Unit One you learned how poets use elements of sound—repetition, rhyme, rhythm, and meter—to create deeper levels of meaning. Listening to the sounds of a poem is essential because the musical qualities of a poem enhance its meaning. Poetry can also appeal to your other senses. In Unit Two you will discover how poetry appeals to your senses to create images that teach you more about life.

You possess a huge reserve of mental pictures and sensations that have been gathered from your experiences and imagination. Those pictures and sensations are stored in your memory, and you can recall them at will. Poets recall their own imaginative memories, summoning specific images through their words and phrases.

A poet may speak of a birch tree bent with snow, a woman's hand touching the keys of a piano, or a drowning man helplessly waving in the sea. Each phrase makes you use your senses in some specific way. The images poets create can surprise, excite, or shock you. They help you perceive the world around you in new ways.

You have learned to listen to poems. Now you will learn to see, feel, and touch poems and to appreciate the ways in which poets use language to create images. By concentrating on precise details and by making unusual comparisons, a poet opens your imagination to his or her particular vision.

In order to understand a poem's imagery, you must read the words and phrases carefully, paying close attention to details. Because poetry is compact, each word or phrase has a purpose. Together, the images, like the sounds, extend the meaning of the poem.

Chapter 4

Selections

Three Haiku:
The Chestnut Burr
Mountain Plum Blossoms
Lightning at Night
MATSUO BASHO

The Locust Tree in Flower
WILLIAM CARLOS WILLIAMS

Living
DENISE LEVERTOV

Lesson   *Images and Imagery*

About the Selections

Many different subjects can inspire poets to write. In earlier chapters you read poems about the death of a loved one, about two friends on a ferry, and about a speaker's memories of his childhood. Identifying the subject of a poem, however, is only the first step to understanding the poem's meaning.

Poets express strong feelings through their poems, often by making you see life or think about the world in a new way. Good poems may show you something you have never seen before or show you a familiar thing in a new guise.

Do all locust trees that flower in spring look alike, or does each tree flower in its own individual way? Is a salamander simply a small animal, or is it actually a creature with unique and fascinating qualities? Those are some of the questions that the poets in this chapter ask you to think about. Nature's beauty, power, and renewal are ideas that have inspired many poets, but as you will see in the poems that follow, each poet expresses those ideas in different ways and with different results.

The first three poems are examples of a traditional Japanese form of poetry called haiku. A <u>haiku</u> is a brief, structured poem composed of seventeen syllables broken into three lines of five, seven, and five syllables. In a haiku the poet lightly sketches an experience by concentrating on a single, central image.

The last two poems in the chapter, "The Locust Tree in Flower" and "Living," also use images of the natural world. Both poems are written in <u>free verse</u>—poetry that does not have any fixed meter, rhyme, or line length. The verse is called "free" because the poet is free to change the patterns or to use no pattern at all. Much twentieth-century poetry is written in free verse.

Matsuo Basho, the author of the three haiku, was born in Japan in 1644. When he was eight years old, he entered the service of a lord and became a close companion of the lord's son. From the son and his tutor, Basho learned about poetry, and he probably wrote his first poem at the age of nine. Basho, who helped to develop the haiku form, is still regarded as one of the greatest haiku poets.

Basho was a prolific writer. Before his death in 1694, he composed over eight hundred poems and a prose work, *The Narrow Road to the Deep North,* which describes a journey he made through northern Japan.

William Carlos Williams, the author of "The Locust Tree in Flower," was born in 1883 in Rutherford, New Jersey. After high school, Williams studied medicine, specializing in pediatrics—the care of children.

Williams wrote poetry, as well as short stories, throughout his life. He was influenced by the imagist movement of poetry, which stressed the importance of using precise observation to present an image. From the ideas of the imagist poets, he developed a personal poetic style based on simplicity and directness. His goal was to see everything he encountered "without forethought and without afterthought but with great intensity of perception."

Williams influenced many later poets, among them Denise Levertov, author of "Living." Levertov was born in 1923 in Essex, England. During World War II, Levertov served as a nurse, and she began publishing her poetry after the war. Her first book, *The Double Image,* appeared in 1946. The following year she met and married an American and moved to the United States.

Levertov credits the move with changing her style. "Marrying an American," she wrote, "and coming here to live while still young was very stimulating to me as a writer for it necessitated the finding of new rhythms in which to write, in accordance with new rhythms of life and speech." Levertov's style, as you will see, mirrors the rhythms of everyday speech. Her images are clear and vivid even though she uses words sparingly.

Lesson Preview

The lesson that follows the poems in this chapter focuses on the imagery in a poem. Imagery refers to all the images, or mental pictures, that are created in a poem.

The poems you will read are all short and the language used in them is simple. To appreciate their imagery, however, you must read them several times. The questions that follow will help you concentrate on the images in the poems. As you read, think about how you would answer these questions.

1 What image is central in each haiku? Is there more than one image in each? What senses (sound, sight, taste, touch, and smell) do the images appeal to?

2 In "The Locust Tree in Flower" what is the speaker describing? Does the image change during the course of the poem?

3 In "Living" what colors are important? What emotions does the speaker feel? How does the title relate to the images in the poem?

Note: The poems in this chapter have no difficult vocabulary.

THREE HAIKU by MATSUO BASHO

Translated by Harold G. Henderson

The Chestnut Burr

The winds of fall
  are blowing, yet how green
    the chestnut burr.

Mountain Plum Blossoms

With the scent of plums
  on the mountain road—suddenly,
    sunrise comes!

Lightning at Night

A lightning gleam:
  into darkness travels
    a night heron's scream.

The Locust Tree in Flower

WILLIAM CARLOS WILLIAMS

Among
of
green

stiff
5 old
bright

broken
branch
come

10 white
sweet
May

again

Living

DENISE LEVERTOV

The fire in leaf and grass
so green it seems
each summer the last summer.

The wind blowing, the leaves
5 shivering in the sun,
each day the last day.

A red salamander
so cold and so
easy to catch, dreamily

10 moves his delicate feet
and long tail. I hold
my hand open for him to go.

Each minute the last minute.

Reviewing the Selections

Answer each of the following questions. You may look back at the poems if necessary.

Recalling Facts

1. "The Chestnut Burr" is set
   - ☐ a. in winter.
   - ☐ b. in the fall.
   - ☐ c. on a snowy day.
   - ☐ d. in the evening.

Understanding Main Ideas

2. "The Locust Tree in Flower" is mainly about a
   - ☐ a. tree beginning to flower in spring.
   - ☐ b. locust tree that is dying.
   - ☐ c. plague of locusts landing on a tree.
   - ☐ d. locust tree standing in a flower bed.

Placing Events in Order

3. In "Living" the speaker frees the salamander
   - ☐ a. before sunrise.
   - ☐ b. before the summer ends.
   - ☐ c. after it gets cold.
   - ☐ d. after feeling it move in her hand.

Finding Supporting Details

4. To how many senses does the poem "Mountain Plum Blossoms" appeal?
   - ☐ a. one
   - ☐ b. two
   - ☐ c. three
   - ☐ d. five

5. "The wind blowing, the leaves / <u>shivering</u> in the sun." In this context *shivering* means
   ☐ a. freezing.
   ☐ b. trembling from fear.
   ☐ c. exploding into thin fragments.
   ☐ d. shaking in the wind.

Interpreting the Selections

Answer each of the following questions. You may look back at the poems if necessary.

6. From "Living" you can infer that the poet
   ☐ a. is dying.
   ☐ b. has never been in the country before.
   ☐ c. feels strongly about nature.
   ☐ d. loves the summer but hates winter.

7. "Mountain Plum Blossoms" takes place
   ☐ a. in spring.
   ☐ b. in winter.
   ☐ c. during a storm.
   ☐ d. after a storm.

8. In "The Locust Tree in Flower" William Carlos Williams uses words such as *green, stiff,* and *broken* to
   ☐ a. tell you that the tree is dead.
   ☐ b. create a clear picture of the locust tree in spring.
   ☐ c. suggest that springtime is full of pain.
   ☐ d. describe the emotional impact that spring has on his senses.

9. Williams's poem and Basho's haiku are similar in that they all
   ☐ a. express a fear of nature.
   ☐ b. reflect a scientific view of nature.
   ☐ c. dramatize a strong preference for life in the country over life in the city.
   ☐ d. try to capture a moment of change in nature.

10. In "Living" the speaker feels an urgent need to
   ☐ a. protect the future of our environment.
   ☐ b. live life "dreamily," like the salamander.
   ☐ c. live life intensely.
   ☐ d. spend as much time as possible outdoors.

Images and Imagery

In Unit One you analyzed how sound contributes to the meaning in a poem. Images are also important to a poem's meaning. As you have learned, images are words or phrases that create pictures in your mind by appealing to any of your senses—sight, sound, taste, smell, and touch.

The most common images in poetry are visual. Poets want you to *see* a scene, an object, a person, or an event in a particular way. If you read closely, however, you will frequently discover that images can appeal to your other senses as well. A word or phrase often conveys impressions to more than one sense at the same time. Think about the phrase *a blazing sun.* It suggests a bright, glaring visual image. Yet the heat from *a blazing sun* also appeals to your sense of touch.

In this lesson you will examine how poets use imagery to create vivid and powerful mental pictures.

Haiku and Imagery

Haiku is a form of poetry developed in Japan in the 1200s. An essential feature of the haiku is its brevity. As you have learned, a haiku consists of seventeen syllables, which are divided into three lines of five, seven, and five syllables. Japanese haiku poets like Matsuo Basho follow that rigid form. The haiku in this lesson, however, do not follow that pattern because they are translations. In translating the poems into English, Harold Henderson was more concerned with finding the best English equivalent of the words than with preserving the exact syllable count.

Scholars do not know exactly how the haiku evolved, although they believe that the form developed from the *tanka,* a poem that was composed of thirty-one syllables divided into lines of five, seven, five, seven, and seven syllables. The first three lines of the tanka are thought to be the basis of the haiku.

Although the first haiku date from the thirteenth century, the form did not become popular until the seventeenth century. Before the time of Basho, haiku often dealt with trivial subjects, such as local gossip. In Basho's work the haiku achieved new richness of meaning.

Because the haiku is very brief, it must create a vivid image. You should instinctively understand the poem without having to apply logical reasoning. The compact form ensures that no unnecessary words complicate the poet's imagery.

Imagery in "The Chestnut Burr." In this haiku Basho translates an experience into images by using <u>concrete language</u>—words that describe things that you know and understand with your senses. Concrete language describes something that actually exists and can be seen or touched in your mind. Concrete nouns in "The Chestnut Burr" include *winds* and *chestnut. Green* is a concrete adjective in the poem.

Basho has captured a moment in autumn in a few concrete words. The poem is effective not only for its vivid images but also for the associations those images call to mind.

1. To what senses does the poem appeal?

2. Many haiku juxtapose, or place side by side, contrasting images. How do the images in "The Chestnut Burr" contrast with each other? What do you associate with the images in the poem?

Imagery in "Mountain Plum Blossoms." Many traditional haiku are written about a specific incident. Place, time, and subject are combined in that incident.

3. Reread "Mountain Plum Blossoms" and identify its place, time, and subject. How do the three work together to re-create a specific incident?

4. What senses are most involved in re-creating the incident?

Imagery in "Lightning at Night." Because a haiku is so compact, each word must evoke a feeling, an idea, or a scene.

5. Reread "Lightning at Night." What do you visualize? What images are juxtaposed? Which of your senses are affected?

6. How does the end of the poem surprise you?

Developing an Image

Like the haiku of Matsuo Basho, "The Locust Tree in Flower" by William Carlos Williams relies on specific images created by concrete language. Each of the adjectives in the poem—*green, stiff, old, bright, broken, sweet*—appeals to one or more of your senses.

The first thing you may notice about the poem is that each line contains only one word, and there is no punctuation. If you try to read the poem as a single sentence, it does not make grammatical sense. Yet the poem is not merely a list of descriptive words. The words are fragments of images, and their arrangement reveals the poet's way of seeing the flowering locust tree.

Williams wants you to think about each individual image. The method he adopts forces you to do that. As you read, you naturally pause at the end of each line.

The speaker imagines the locust tree in bloom, but instead of describing its general appearance, he examines each concrete detail of the tree. Williams isolates his impressions—one word for each line, one line for each word. By doing so, he emphasizes the importance of each impression. You identify the concrete details and slowly build a complete image.

7. How does the physical appearance of the poem suggest growth?

Imagery and Mood

In the last poem, "Living," Denise Levertov uses concrete language to establish the mood of her poem. Mood, as you have learned, is the general feeling or atmosphere in a poem. The mood of "Living" is supported by Levertov's appeal to your senses.

8. What are the main images in "Living," and to what sense or senses does each appeal?

The poet uses her images to create the mood. The mood is centered in the quiet, intense excitement that the speaker feels about life. Read the first stanza of the poem.

> The fire in leaf and grass
> so green it seems
> each summer the last summer.

The speaker is not describing a real fire. What he or she sees and feels is the deep, rich green of "leaf and grass." That quality is so intense that "leaf and grass" seem to be on fire, ablaze with life.

9. Choose another strong image in the poem and describe how it reflects the mood of the poem.

Everything in the poem is felt strongly, even the "delicate feet" of the salamander against the speaker's hand. That depth of feeling is reinforced by the speaker's insistence that each summer, each day, and each minute may be the last. The repeated references to time are like a refrain.

10. How do the references to time change during the course of the poem? What does the change reflect about the emotional state of the speaker?

11. Think about the meaning of the poem's title. According to the speaker, what is true living?

12. Like the haiku, "Living" is extremely emotional. How is it similar to or different from the emotions in the haiku?

Questions for Thought and Discussion

The questions and activities that follow will help you explore the poems in this chapter in more depth and at the same time develop your critical thinking skills.

1. **Expressing an Opinion.** One critic has written that Basho "attempted to compress the meaning of the world into the simple pattern of his poetry." Do you agree with this judgment? Why or why not?

Images and Imagery

2. **Comparing.** All the poems in this chapter use images from nature. Compare and contrast the poets' imagery. For example, how does Basho's imagery resemble Levertov's? How does Levertov's vision of nature differ from Williams's observations?

3. **Recognizing Contrasting Images.** In "Living" Denise Levertov uses a variety of contrasting images. Explain how the poet mixes hot/cold and quickness/slowness. What do those contrasts add to the meaning of the poem?

4. **Identifying a Poem's Mood.** Choose one of Basho's haiku and identify its mood. Support your answer with evidence from the poem.

5. **Generalizing.** Reread the three haiku. What general ideas about the natural world do all three express?

Writing About Literature

Several suggestions for writing projects are given below. You may be asked to complete one or more of these projects. If you have any questions about how to begin a writing assignment, review Using the Writing Process, beginning on page 219.

1. **Composing a Haiku.** Write a haiku based on an experience in your own life. Choose an object or a scene that evokes a strong emotional response in you. Use concrete language to build specific images. Try to juxtapose contrasting images, using one image to say something about the other. Use Basho's haiku as models.

2. **Writing a Description Using Imagery.** Write a description of a person, a place, or a thing using images that appeal to each of the five senses. The description may be in prose or poetry. The description should be brief yet precise.

3. **Translating an Abstract Idea into Concrete Images.** Think of an abstract idea, such as freedom, or a quality, such as truth, honesty, or loyalty. Then write a poem in which you translate that idea or quality into concrete images.

Chapter 5

Selections

I Am Not Yours
SARA TEASDALE

Not Waving but Drowning
STEVIE SMITH

Sonnet 116:
Let Me Not to the Marriage of True Minds
WILLIAM SHAKESPEARE

Lesson *Figurative Language*

About the Selections

Sometimes a straightforward statement seems inadequate for explaining a thought or a feeling. You may know what you want to say or how you feel, but you might have difficulty expressing yourself. To find the right words, you search for an example—an object, a situation, an idea, or an image that is similar to what you are thinking or feeling. By using a comparison, you can often communicate your meaning more clearly. You might say, for example, "George is like a bear in the morning." The comparison suggests that George, like a bear, is cross and easily angered. When you compare George and the bear, you get a strong visual image of George's behavior.

The use of comparisons to convey and enrich meaning is at the heart of poetry. Good poets are masters of imaginative comparison. Often the comparisons they make give you new and surprising ways of looking at and understanding life.

The poems in this chapter illustrate how poets create images and extend the meanings of their poems through comparisons. In "I Am Not Yours" Sara Teasdale expresses the overwhelming feelings of intense love. In "Not Waving but Drowning" Stevie Smith portrays a man who has lived a life of desperation.

Finally, in Sonnet 116, "Let Me Not to the Marriage of True Minds," William Shakespeare makes a number of comparisons that express the speaker's feelings about the timelessness of true love.

Sara Teasdale, the author of the first poem, was born in St. Louis, Missouri, in 1884. She attended private schools, and at an early age she traveled extensively. As a young woman, she frequently visited Chicago, where she met other poets and began to publish her own poems in magazines. She rejected a proposal of marriage from the poet Vachel Lindsay and married a St. Louis businessman in 1914. Lonely and withdrawn after her divorce in 1929, she committed suicide in 1933.

Sara Teasdale was one of the most popular poets of the early twentieth century, winning the Pulitzer Prize for poetry in 1917. She wrote short, delicate, and intensely personal poems. Because they are drawn from her own experience, they have been called autobiographical. Love, beauty, and death are themes in many of her works.

Stevie Smith (1902–1971) is the pen name of Florence Margaret Smith. She was born in Hull, England, and grew up in a suburb of London. She worked for a London publisher for several years. Smith spent most of her life living with an aunt until the woman's death at the age of ninety-six.

In the 1960s Stevie Smith began to give poetry readings at schools across Britain and was such a success that she was asked to read on radio and to make recordings. Smith's poems, which often concern death and loneliness, are a striking mixture of seriousness and humor. Smith also wrote novels, short stories, and essays.

The third poem, "Let Me Not to the Marriage of True Minds," was written almost four hundred years ago. Its author, William Shakespeare, is recognized as one of the greatest poets and playwrights to have written in English. For a writer of such importance, surprisingly little is known about him.

William Shakespeare (1564–1616) was born in the small English town of Stratford-upon-Avon, and he probably lived there until he was in his twenties. About 1590, he joined a company of actors who performed plays in London. As far as anyone now knows, he was never a leading actor, but he quickly became the company's most successful playwright.

In 1609, toward the end of his career, a book of 154 of his sonnets was published. All the sonnets are love poems and are dedicated to a mysterious person identified only by initials. Most people agree that the sonnets are among

Shakespeare's finest poems. The poem you will read in this chapter is Sonnet 116. Because Shakespeare did not give his sonnets titles, they are often referred to by the words of their first lines. Sonnet 116 is also known as "Let Me Not to the Marriage of True Minds."

Lesson Preview

The lesson that follows examines the imaginative comparisons that poets use in their works. Poets suggest ideas and feelings by comparing dissimilar words and phrases. Those imaginative comparisons create connotations beyond the usual meanings of those words and phrases.

Each of the poems in this chapter treats a serious subject. Two are about love and one concerns death. In all three poems the poets use comparisons to enhance meaning. The questions that follow will help you identify those comparisons and understand the special ways in which the poets use language. As you read, think about how you would answer these questions.

1 In "I Am Not Yours" what does the speaker want? What comparison or comparisons does the poet use?

2 In "Not Waving but Drowning" who is speaking? What kind of life did the man live? What is his life compared to?

3 According to Shakespeare, what is the nature of true love? Does it ever change?

4 What images does Shakespeare use to express his ideas?

Vocabulary

Here are some difficult words that appear in Sonnet 116. Study the words and their definitions, as well as the sentences that show how the words are used. This will help you get the most from your reading.

tempest a violent storm with high winds. *While we were camping, an unexpected tempest blew our tent into the lake and left us drenched by a downpour.*

impediments obstacles. *Poor families often find that high prices and crowded clinics are impediments to receiving health care.*

bark a small boat. *The boys set sail in a bark they had made from wooden crates.*

I Am Not Yours

SARA TEASDALE

I am not yours, not lost in you,
    Not lost, although I long to be
Lost as a candle lit at noon,
    Lost as a snowflake in the sea.

5   You love me, and I find you still
    A spirit beautiful and bright,
Yet I am I, who long to be
    Lost as a light is lost in light.

Oh plunge me deep in love—put out
10   My senses, leave me deaf and blind,
Swept by the tempest of your love,
    A taper[1] in a rushing wind.

---

1. **taper:** long, slender candle.

Not Waving but Drowning

STEVIE SMITH

Nobody heard him, the dead man,
But still he lay moaning:
I was much further out than you thought
And not waving but drowning.

5 Poor chap, he always loved larking[1]
   And now he's dead
   It must have been too cold for him his heart gave way,
   They said.

   Oh, no no no, it was too cold always
10 (Still the dead one lay moaning)
   I was much too far out all my life
   And not waving but drowning.

---

1. larking: having a merry time.

Sonnet 116:
Let Me Not to the Marriage of True Minds

WILLIAM SHAKESPEARE

Let me not to the marriage of true minds
Admit impediments;[1] love is not love
Which alters when it alteration finds
Or bends with the remover to remove.[2]
5 O, no, it is an ever-fixèd mark[3]
That looks on tempests and is never shaken;
It is the star to every wand'ring bark,
Whose worth's unknown, although his height[4] be taken.

---

1. Admit impediments: those words recall the line in the traditional marriage service in which a minister asks if either party knows of any impediment, or hindrance, as to why they may not be lawfully joined together in matrimony. **2. bends . . . remove:** changes with a fickle lover. **3. mark:** refers to a sea mark—a prominent object on shore, such as a lighthouse, that serves as a guide for ships. **4. his height:** the star's distance.

Love's not Time's fool,[5] though rosy lips and cheeks
10 Within his bending sickle's compass come;[6]
Love alters not with his brief hours and weeks,
But bears it out[7] even to the edge of doom.

    If this be error, and upon me proved,
    I never writ, nor no man ever loved.

---

5. fool: plaything. **6. Within . . . compass:** Here Shakespeare is speaking
of the passing of time. Time is often portrayed as an old man with a
sickle—a harvesting tool having a long curved blade. Anything coming
within the compass, or range, of the sickle would be cut down by
time. **7. bears it out:** persists.

Reviewing the Selections

Answer each of the following questions. You may look back at the poems if necessary.

Recalling Facts

1. In "I Am Not Yours" the speaker uses all the following images *except* a
   ☐ a. candle lit in daylight.
   ☐ b. snowflake in water.
   ☐ c. snowflake in summer.
   ☐ d. candle in a wind.

Understanding Main Ideas

2. The speaker in "I Am Not Yours" wants to
   ☐ a. marry and have children.
   ☐ b. be overwhelmed by love.
   ☐ c. get lost at sea during a tempest.
   ☐ d. become the best poet in the world.

Placing Events in Order

3. In "Not Waving but Drowning" the man died
   ☐ a. before anyone saw him.
   ☐ b. after he was brought to shore.
   ☐ c. after asking his friends for help.
   ☐ d. after trying to signal his distress.

Finding Supporting Details

4. In "Let Me Not to the Marriage of True Minds," the speaker argues that true love never changes. What does alter with time?
   ☐ a. the position of the stars
   ☐ b. the ferocity of tempests
   ☐ c. a lover's rosy lips and cheeks
   ☐ d. a poet's energy and imagination

5. "Let me not to the marriage of true minds / Admit impediments; love is not love / Which alters when it <u>alteration</u> finds." In this context *alteration* means

☐ a. change.

☐ b. argument.

☐ c. adoration.

☐ d. resistance.

Interpreting the Selections

Answer each of the following questions. You may look back at the poems if necessary.

6. In "I Am Not Yours" the speaker

☐ a. has never been in love before.

☐ b. is afraid of becoming deaf and blind.

☐ c. has learned to distrust love.

☐ d. knows the power of love.

7. In "Not Waving but Drowning" what generalization can you make about the people who observe the dead man?

☐ a. They never really understood him.

☐ b. They were his friends and loved him well.

☐ c. They despised him and were unaffected by his death.

☐ d. They looked on him as an unhappy person.

8. In "Not Waving but Drowning" the poet suggests
    that the man had
    - ☐ a. suffered greatly throughout his life.
    - ☐ b. enjoyed life to the fullest.
    - ☐ c. preferred risking death to living a dull life.
    - ☐ d. always known that one day he would
      drown at sea.

9. The poems by Teasdale and Shakespeare are both
    about love, yet they are very different from each
    other. One difference is that
    - ☐ a. Shakespeare's poem is more emotional.
    - ☐ b. only Teasdale's poem has visual images.
    - ☐ c. Teasdale's poem is more personal
      and immediate.
    - ☐ d. only Shakespeare's poem is about
      romantic love.

10. From reading "Let Me Not to the Marriage of
    True Minds," what conclusion can you draw
    about the speaker's attitude toward love?
    - ☐ a. It is cynical.
    - ☐ b. It is idealistic.
    - ☐ c. It is unromantic.
    - ☐ d. It is sentimental.

Figurative Language

Comparisons are a part of everyday language. You use them in conversation to clarify and reinforce your feelings and ideas. Poets also use comparisons. They draw comparisons not only to clarify meaning but also to surprise, to enlighten, and to deepen your understanding of an idea or an emotion.

Many of the comparisons in poetry involve figurative language. Figurative language refers to words and phrases used in unusual ways to create strong, vivid images, to focus attention on certain ideas, or to compare things that are basically different. When words or phrases are used figuratively, they have meanings other than their usual, or literal, meanings. If, for example, someone asks you to "lend a hand," he or she does not literally want to borrow your hand. Instead, the expression represents an idea—the idea of joining in to help.

Figurative language is composed of specific constructions called figures of speech. A figure of speech is a word or phrase that creates a vivid image by contrasting unlike things. A figure of speech compares an object, an action, or a feeling with something else. "I slept like a log," "He ran like the wind," and "She has the face of an angel" are common figures of speech. In fact, they have been used so often that they have become clichés—outworn expressions that no longer express an original idea. Poets avoid overused figures of speech and try to create fresh images.

Simile

There are many kinds of figures of speech, but among the most important are similes, metaphors, and personification. A simile is a direct comparison between two unlike things that are connected by the word *like, as,* or *resembles* or the verb *appears* or *seems.* The purpose of a simile is to give you a new way of looking at one of the things. "He ran like the wind" is an example of a simile. Sara Teasdale uses similes in "I Am Not Yours."

The speaker in "I Am Not Yours" is deeply in love and regrets the separation between herself and her beloved.

> I am not yours, not lost in you,
> Not lost, although I long to be

In line 3 the speaker declares that she longs to be "Lost as a candle lit at noon." That simile creates an unusual visual image of a candle burning in bright daylight. The light from the candle is absorbed into the daylight, just as the speaker wants to be absorbed into her lover. That simile also suggests another sensory image.

1. To what sense, other than sight, does the simile appeal? How is that image well suited to the speaker's passion?

2. Find another simile in the first stanza. What image does it create? What feeling or feelings does the image suggest?

Metaphor

Another important figure of speech—the one most often used in poetry—is the metaphor. A metaphor is an imaginative implied comparison between two unlike things. A metaphor is a comparison that suggests that one thing *is* another. If you describe a person by saying "She's a tiger," you are using a metaphor to compare that human being to a wild animal. You are also giving her all the feelings and associations surrounding the word *tiger.* You are suggesting that she is ferocious, aggressive, and powerful.

3. Read line 7 of Shakespeare's "Let Me Not to the Marriage of True Minds." What is the metaphor in that line? Reread the beginning of the poem to discover what "it" refers to. What image does the metaphor suggest? How is the metaphor developed in line 8?

Implicit Metaphor in "I Am Not Yours." In some metaphors poets speak of one thing as though it were another without stating the comparison for you. An implicit metaphor is a special kind of metaphor in which one of the terms is not stated but suggested by the context. "The children flocked to the ice cream stand" is an example of an implicit metaphor in which the children are indirectly compared to sheep by the word *flocked*.

There are two examples of implicit metaphors in Sara Teasdale's poem "I Am Not Yours." In line 11 the speaker desires to be "Swept by the tempest of your [her lover's] love." The implicit metaphor indirectly compares her lover's emotions to a tempest, or a violent storm. The metaphor evokes images of turbulence and power, connotations associated with the word *tempest,* and reinforces the speaker's image of the force of her lover's feelings.

4. Reread the last stanza of "I Am Not Yours," paying particular attention to the implicit metaphor in the last line. What things are compared in that implicit metaphor?

Implicit Metaphor in "Not Waving but Drowning." Stevie Smith's "Not Waving but Drowning" also contains an implicit metaphor. The key to discovering the implicit metaphor lies in understanding the meaning of the poem.

The poem is not difficult to understand if you identify its setting and recognize who the speakers are. The references to drowning tell you that the setting is near a body of water. A dead man is lying on the shore.

5. Reread "Not Waving but Drowning" and identify the speakers.

Both speakers make several observations about the dead man's life. You learn that even though "he always loved larking," the man was "not waving but drowning." The drowning was not an unexpected event; the water was *always* too cold.

> I was much too far out all my life
> And not waving but drowning.

6. Identify the implicit metaphor. What do you learn about the dead man's life? How did others see him? How did he see himself?

7. Once you understand the implicit metaphor, what new meaning does the first line assume?

Personification

In "Let Me Not to the Marriage of True Minds," Shakespeare argues that true love is constant and changeless. He enlarges on that idea through a series of metaphors and through another figure of speech called personification. Personification is a figure of speech in which an animal, an object, or an idea is given human qualities. Perhaps you have heard the phrase "The sun smiled on the land." In that phrase the sun is personified—it smiles, which is a human ability. Poets often use personification to describe abstract ideas such as freedom, truth, and beauty.

Shakespeare uses personification to speak about both love and time. Reread line 9 carefully. Notice that Shakespeare speaks of love as not being "Time's fool." Personification gives love the ability to determine whether or not to be a fool.

Poets and artists have often personified the idea of time. Illustrations frequently show time as a bent, white-haired old man holding a sickle. As you may know, a sickle is a tool with a curved blade that was once used by farmers to harvest grain. Time's sickle is a symbol of death—a reminder that time eventually "cuts" everyone down. Shakespeare, too, portrays an image of time with a sickle. In lines 9 and 10 he creates an image of time cutting down the "rosy lips and cheeks" of lovers with its blade.

8. According to the poem, what is the relationship between love and time? How does the personification of the two ideas add to the meaning of the poem?

Figurative Language and A Sonnet

"Let Me Not to the Marriage of True Minds" is an example of a particular kind of poem called a sonnet. A sonnet is a fourteen-line poem with a fixed pattern or rhythm and meter. The lines are usually in iambic pentameter. Sonnets usually treat a single idea, and many deal with some aspect of love.

Because of their fixed form, sonnets depend on figurative language to develop ideas and create images. Sonnet 116, for example, relies on imaginative metaphors and the personification of abstract ideas to create meaning in the poem.

There are two basic types of sonnet: the Italian, or Petrarchan, sonnet and the Shakespearean sonnet, often referred to as the English sonnet. Each has its own structure and rhyme scheme. The Italian sonnet is divided into two parts, the first having eight lines and the second having six lines. The Shakespearean sonnet is composed of three <u>quatrains</u>, or four-line stanzas, and a concluding couplet of two rhyming lines.

The Shakespearean sonnet bears Shakespeare's name because he used the form so frequently and skillfully. In a Shakespearean sonnet the three quatrains introduce and examine the central idea. In the concluding couplet the poet summarizes or comments on that idea. The rhyme scheme of a Shakespearean sonnet *(abab cdcd efef gg)* reflects the progressive development of ideas.

9. What is the central idea of Sonnet 116? What comment does the concluding couplet make?

Questions for Thought and Discussion

The questions and activities that follow will help you explore the three poems in this chapter in more depth and at the same time develop your critical thinking skills.

1. **Analyzing Figurative Language.** Review what you learned about Sara Teasdale's use of the candle simile in "I Am Not Yours." Then look at the last line of the poem. How has she changed that simile into a metaphor? What feelings does that suggest?

2. **Interpreting.** Reread "Not Waving but Drowning." What does the poet think about the dead man and the others who observe him? What view of human nature is implied in her view of the dead man? What view of human relationships and society is implied in her depiction of the other people?

3. **Analyzing Character.** In "Not Waving but Drowning" what kind of life had the dead man lived? How was he perceived by others? How well did that perception correspond to reality? Support your answers with evidence from the poem.

4. **Identifying Metaphors.** In small groups study Shakespeare's sonnet "Let Me Not to the Marriage of True Minds." How many metaphors do you find

in the poem? Choose one metaphor and explain its meaning to the class, describing what two things are compared and what the comparison suggests.

5. **Expressing an Opinion.** Shakespeare's theme is the constancy of true love. Do you agree or disagree with Shakespeare's argument that love, if it is true, cannot waver in the face of obstacles or time? Give reasons for your opinions.

Writing About Literature

Several suggestions for writing projects are given below. You may be asked to complete one or more of these projects. If you have any questions about how to begin a writing assignment, review Using the Writing Process, beginning on page 219.

1. **Comparing Imagery.** All three poems in this chapter contain sea imagery. Write several paragraphs in which you compare the use of sea imagery in each poem. Explain what the sea represents in each poem. How does each poet use the image of the sea differently and similarly? Discuss why you think the sea can be used to mean so many different things.

2. **Analyzing Figurative Language.** Choose a poem in an earlier chapter and analyze the poet's use of figurative language. Discuss what figures of speech are used, what each figure of speech means, and how the figurative language helps to express the theme of the poem.

3. **Creating an Extended Metaphor.** Write a few lines of poetry or a paragraph of prose in which you create and develop a metaphor that expresses a feeling or an idea. First decide on the feeling or the idea you want to communicate. Then think of an object, an action, or an idea that evokes an image that relates to your feeling or idea. Create a metaphor by comparing the two things in an imaginative way.

4. **Paraphrasing a Poem.** A paraphrase is a restatement in your own words of part or all of a written work. Paraphrasing a poem is a good way of understanding the poem thoroughly. Paraphrase "Let Me Not to the Marriage of True Minds," expressing each specific point of the poem in your own words.

Figurative Language

Chapter 6

Selections

The Secret Heart
ROBERT P. TRISTRAM COFFIN

The Song of Wandering Aengus
WILLIAM BUTLER YEATS

Lesson

Imagery, Metaphor, and Symbols

About the Selections

Your imagination is constantly active. Imagination not only creates your dreams, daydreams, fantasies, and nightmares but also colors your memories. You may recall some memories vividly, but notice that others have changed or faded away. Perhaps you have wondered whether a remembered event happened or whether it was actually a dream.

Poets depend on various aspects of imagination, as well as on memories, to inspire their poems. From those sources, they create works that are unique, full of detail, and rich in feeling. Memories, dreams, and fantasies play important roles in the two poems in this chapter.

Robert P. Tristram Coffin (1892–1955), who wrote "The Secret Heart," was born in Brunswick, Maine, and grew up along the Maine coast. In 1911 Coffin entered Bowdoin College. Later, he did graduate work in literature at Princeton University and at Oxford University, in England. During World War I he served as an artillery officer. After completing his studies at Oxford in 1920, Coffin returned to the United States and began a distinguished academic career teaching literature.

Coffin wrote fiction, essays, biography, history, and criticism, but he is chiefly remembered for his poetry. A strong current of religious feeling is evident throughout his work. "Coffin's voice, even at its most personal, is always a public voice revealing God," wrote one critic.

Coffin loved ordinary, everyday things, and he once noted, "I had the mistaken idea that a poet must always be on the mountain top. Only in maturity did I learn to come down on the plain and choose for my poems the simple subjects of everyday."

William Butler Yeats, the author of "The Song of Wandering Aengus," is considered one of the greatest poets in the English language. He was born near Dublin, Ireland, in 1865, but he spent a great deal of time in Sligo, a county to the west. The landscapes around Sligo inspired many of his poems.

Yeats's work is rich and complex, reflecting the varied interests that influenced him. As a young writer, he was drawn to magic and mysticism as well as to Irish folklore and legend. Intrigued by history, he formulated his own theories about history as a recurring cycle of events. He describes those theories in an elaborate book called *A Vision*.

Yeats's writing was also inspired by his love for Maude Gonne, an Irish nationalist leader who liked and admired Yeats but did not return his love. Many of his love poems were written for her, and she was the model for several characters in his plays.

Yeats was a leading figure in the Irish literary renaissance, a movement of the late 1800s and early 1900s. The writers involved in the movement sought to revive interest in traditional Irish literature, folklore, and legends to encourage new works that reflected Irish history and culture. Many members supported the famous Abbey Theatre which Yeats helped to found and direct. His own plays, as well as those of other Irish writers, were produced there.

In 1923 Yeats was awarded the Nobel Prize for literature. Now a very famous man, he continued his active involvement in Irish political and cultural life. Some of his best work was written in the ten years before his death in 1939.

Lesson Preview

The lesson that follows the two poems focuses on the relationship between imagery, metaphor, and symbols. By closely examining these elements in a poem, you can understand the poem's theme, or underlying message, more clearly.

The questions that follow will help you identify some important elements in the two poems. As you read, think about how you would answer these questions.

1 What image or images are at the center of "The Secret Heart"? How are the images compared to one another?

2 What does the boy in "The Secret Heart" actually see? How does it come to stand for something else?

3 What do you think the title "The Secret Heart " means?

4 What is the setting (the time and place) of "The Song of Wandering Aengus"? What is the plot, or sequence of events, of the poem? What images do you see in the poem?

5 What does the speaker in "The Song of Wandering Aengus" want after he sees the girl? How do his wishes and actions stand for something beyond their actual meanings?

Vocabulary

Here are some difficult words that appear in the poems that follow. Study the words and their definitions, as well as the sentences that show how the words are used. This will help you get the most from your reading.

sire father. *The sire of this champion racehorse also won many races when he was younger.*

semblance likeness. *Because she didn't want to go to school, the child created a semblance of illness by complaining of stomach pains.*

The Secret Heart

ROBERT P. TRISTRAM COFFIN

Across the years he could recall
His father one way best of all.

In the stillest hour of night
The boy awakened to a light.

5   Half in dreams, he saw his sire
With his great hands full of fire.

The man had struck a match to see
If his son slept peacefully.

He held his palms each side the spark
10   His love had kindled in the dark.

His two hands were curved apart
In the semblance of a heart.

He wore, it seemed to his small son,
A bare heart on his hidden one,

15   A heart that gave out such a glow
No son awake could bear to know.

It showed a look upon a face
Too tender for the day to trace.

One instant, it lit all about,
20   And then the secret heart went out.

But it shone long enough for one
To know that hands held up the sun.

The Song of Wandering Aengus

WILLIAM BUTLER YEATS

I went out to the hazel wood,
Because a fire was in my head,
And cut and peeled a hazel wand,
And hooked a berry to a thread;
5 And when white moths were on the wing,
And moth-like stars were flickering out,
I dropped the berry in a stream
And caught a little silver trout.

When I had laid it on the floor
10 I went to blow the fire aflame,
But something rustled on the floor,
And some one called me by my name:
It had become a glimmering girl
With apple blossom in her hair
15 Who called me by my name and ran
And faded through the brightening air.

Though I am old with wandering
Through hollow lands and hilly lands,
I will find out where she has gone,
20 And kiss her lips and take her hands;
And walk among long dappled grass,
And pluck till time and times are done
The silver apples of the moon,
The golden apples of the sun.

Reviewing the Selections

Answer each of the following questions. You may look back at the poems if necessary.

Recalling Facts

1. In "The Secret Heart" the boy awakens
   ☐ a. just as the sun rises.
   ☐ b. in the middle of the night.
   ☐ c. during an afternoon nap.
   ☐ d. just as he is falling asleep.

Understanding Main Ideas

2. In "The Secret Heart" the father stands over his son because
   ☐ a. he wants to talk to the boy about their shared memories.
   ☐ b. the boy has cried out in his sleep.
   ☐ c. the boy has been ill and the father is worried.
   ☐ d. he loves his son and wants to see that he is sleeping peacefully.

Placing Events in Order

3. In "The Song of Wandering Aengus" what happens after the speaker goes to fan the flame of the fire?
   ☐ a. The fish he has caught changes into a beautiful girl.
   ☐ b. The fish seems to cry out in a human voice.
   ☐ c. A mermaid appears before him on the shore.
   ☐ d. It begins to rain, and he cannot start the fire.

Finding Supporting Details

4. In Yeats's poem the speaker's fishing rod is made of
   ☐ a. dogwood, string, and a nail.
   ☐ b. a pine stick, thread, silver apples, and a pin.
   ☐ c. a silver cane with a berry on the end of it.
   ☐ d. hazel wood, thread, a hook, and a berry.

5. "He held his palms each side the spark / His love had <u>kindled</u> in the dark." In this context *kindled* means

   ☐ a. extinguished.

   ☐ b. increased.

   ☐ c. ignited.

   ☐ d. imagined.

Interpreting the Selections

Answer each of the following questions. You may look back at the poems if necessary.

6. In "The Secret Heart" the speaker probably remembers this incident from his childhood because

   ☐ a. it presented a powerful image of his father's love for him.

   ☐ b. his father died soon afterward.

   ☐ c. he was terrified by the experience of waking up and seeing the fire in his father's hands.

   ☐ d. he and his father often spoke about the incident afterward.

7. What statement can you make about the setting of "The Song of Wandering Aengus"?

   ☐ a. It shows everyday life on an Irish farm.

   ☐ b. It is an urban and briskly modern setting.

   ☐ c. It suggests a magical and mysterious place.

   ☐ d. The poem probably takes place on another planet.

8. Yeats used the word *I* in his poem to
   - ☐ a. make the story seem more immediate.
   - ☐ b. make the poem sound more Irish.
   - ☐ c. prove that Aengus was a real person.
   - ☐ d. show that love can profoundly affect
     a person.

9. Think about the mood of the two poems. In what
   ways are the moods alike?
   - ☐ a. Both cast a romantic look at the past.
   - ☐ b. Both present stern and practical views.
   - ☐ c. Both poems describe events in a dreamlike
     and magical way.
   - ☐ d. Both poems express a deep sense of loss.

10. In "The Secret Heart" the boy imagines that his
    father's hands are "full of fire" because
    - ☐ a. his father is holding a silver lantern.
    - ☐ b. his father is building a fire in the fireplace.
    - ☐ c. the boy is having a nightmare about the
      house catching on fire.
    - ☐ d. his father is holding a lighted match.

Imagery, Metaphor, and Symbols

To understand fully the meaning of a poem, it is often necessary to read the poem two or three times. Each time you read it, the meaning becomes clearer, and various levels of meaning are often revealed.

Most poems can be understood on more than one level. The first level—the surface level—is the most obvious. On that level, words carry their ordinary denotations, or dictionary meanings. You identify the speaker, the subject, and the mood of the poem. The poem may also have a setting and a plot. In your first reading of a poem, you will usually discover its surface level, but most poems have deeper meanings as well. In order to understand those other levels of meaning you need to study the poet's images and figurative language.

Sometimes a single image suggests that the poem has multiple meanings. At other times, a poet may use a series of images to develop additional meanings. Often knowing about the poet's interests and beliefs helps you to recognize other levels of meaning in his or her work.

Each of the poems in this chapter can be understood on more than one level. In this lesson you will learn how imagery, metaphor, and symbols deepen the meaning of each poem.

"The Secret Heart": Reading for Meaning

On the surface, Coffin's "The Secret Heart" is a straightforward poem. The speaker is standing outside the action and telling the story from the vantage point of *he*. The speaker describes a single scene—a vivid recollection of an incident in childhood.

1. Why do you think Coffin uses he *instead of* I*?*

In the poem the speaker recalls a special moment with his father. As a child, very late one night, he is awakened by a light. Still half asleep, he looks up and sees his father. The father has lit a match to see if the child is sleeping well. He cups the match in both hands and holds up the flame. Because of the way the father holds the light in his hands, the boy imagines that his father is holding a glowing heart in front of his real, hidden heart.

> He wore, it seemed to his small son,
> A bare heart on his hidden one,

2. Think about the images the poet creates: the father's "bare heart" and "his hidden one." To what sense or senses do those images appeal?

Developing a Metaphor

The poet begins the poem with a simple image: two hands holding a lighted match. Coffin then extends the image into a metaphor. As you learned in Chapter 5, a metaphor is an indirect comparison between two unlike things. One thing assumes the qualities of the other, so that it seems to *become* the other.

In "The Secret Heart" the father's hands cupped around the flame seem to form a human heart. Think about all the feelings and ideas that *heart* connotes—life, love, warmth, and happiness.

3. What does the metaphor in this poem suggest about the human heart?

Developing a Symbol

From line 15 until the end of the poem, Coffin develops the metaphor into a symbol. A <u>symbol</u> is a person, a place, or an object that stands for something other or more important than itself. A symbol can be a situation or an action as well as an individual person, place, or object.

Symbols often stand for ideas or qualities. If you have ever saluted the flag, stopped at a traffic light, studied a road map, or avoided a black cat, then you have recognized and responded to a symbol. To Americans, the colors red, white, and blue symbolize, or stand for, their nation. A red light symbolizes stop. A star on a road map symbolizes a large city. A black cat traditionally symbolizes bad luck.

4. Name two or three other common symbols and identify what is symbolized by each.

Symbols are often used in poetry. A symbol may appear only once in a poem, or it may reappear throughout the poem. Symbols allow a poet to take advantage of the connotations, or associations, of words. Symbols also enrich a poem, intensifying a feeling or focusing on a particular idea.

The meaning of "The Secret Heart" is developed through a progression of image, metaphor, and symbol. The poet first introduces the image of hands holding a lighted match in the dark, then compares that image to the human heart, and finally develops the metaphor into a symbol of love.

The symbolism continues to develop in the last stanza. The final two lines suggest a love even greater than that between the father and his child. For a moment, the child becomes aware not only of his father's love for him but also of a higher love—of God's love for humanity. As the father's hands held the flame of a match, God's "hands held up the sun." As the father loves the child, God loves humankind.

5. How does the title of "The Secret Heart" contribute to its symbolism?

Symbolism and Allusion

"The Song of Wandering Aengus" also contains symbols. Its symbolism, however, is related to the poet's use of allusion. <u>Allusion</u> is a reference to something real or fictitious outside the poem. Poets frequently allude, or refer, to Biblical figures and events. Allusions to the gods of Greek and Roman mythology, such as Apollo and Jupiter, also appear in many poems.

An allusion is a kind of comparison. It suggests a connection between the poet's own idea and the outside reference which he or she is making. An allusion allows a poet to mention something without including a detailed explanation, because he or she assumes you will recognize the allusion. For example, if a poet alludes to Romeo and Juliet when writing about two people in love, you immediately understand that the lovers are young, their love faces strong opposition, and that their story ends tragically. The poet does not need to provide that information for you. Allusions make poetry a compact literary form, because they compress ideas and create strong images.

6. List several people, places, or events that are commonly recognized as representing certain ideas or feelings. Explain the symbolic importance of your choices.

Yeats's Use of Allusion

William Butler Yeats was intrigued by Irish folklore and mythology. He studied the stories of the Celtic gods and heroes. In those stories he discovered what he considered to be the true Irish spirit. As you learned in the introduction to this lesson, Yeats felt that modern Irish writers should create works that would renew the ancient heroic tradition.

"The Song of Wandering Aengus" is one of Yeats's early poems. Many of his early works allude to Celtic mythology and to Irish folklore, as well as to classical Greek and Roman mythology. "The Song of Wandering Aengus" borrows from several myths and folktales.

A common element of many Irish stories is the sudden appearance before a man of a beautiful and mysterious woman. When the man approaches the woman, she vanishes. The man is enchanted by the vision and for the rest of his life, he searches in vain for the woman.

In "The Song of Wandering Aengus" Yeats creates his own version of that story. The name Aengus (AHN guhs) is an allusion to Celtic mythology. Aengus was the Celtic god of love, beauty, and poetry. Because the poem is written in the first person, you can assume that the speaker is Aengus himself.

7. Briefly summarize the plot of the poem.

8. How is the poem similar to at least one idea common to many traditional Irish folktales?

Interpreting Symbols

"The Song of Wandering Aengus" tells a magical story of timeless love. Like many folktales, its setting is an imaginary place where supernatural events are common. You can read and enjoy the poem on that level alone. Yet the poem has a deeper symbolic meaning.

Identifying the symbolism lies in remembering that the original Aengus was the god of love, beauty, and poetry. Thus, Yeats's Aengus can symbolize all poets. In the poem the speaker, "wandering Aengus," searches for the "glimmering girl" he once saw. Aengus seeks the girl the same way poets seek beauty and truth.

Remember that a symbol can also be an action or a series of actions or events. In the poem Aengus is a wanderer, a man in search of something. Although Aengus sees the girl for only a moment, the vision of her beauty inspires him all his life. Having seen beauty, Aengus will never stop looking for it. Aengus's search for the woman symbolizes the quest for beauty that has always inspired poets.

9. Aengus says that he went to the wood because "a fire was in my head." What does that mean? How might the description apply to a poet's experience?

10. Reread stanza 1, paying careful attention to the specific actions described. How are Aengus's actions similar to those of a poet at work?

11. The silver trout changes into "a glimmering girl" and vanishes. For a poet, what might the sudden appearance of the woman symbolize?

Questions for Thought and Discussion

The questions and activities that follow will help you explore the poems in this chapter in more depth and at the same time develop your critical thinking skills.

1. **Interpreting the Theme.** As a class, develop a statement that summarizes the theme of "The Secret Heart." As you do so, keep in mind the various levels of meaning in the poem. For example, in what sense is the poem about the power of love? The existence of God? The relationship between God and humanity?

2. **Analyzing Symbolism.** In the lesson you studied the symbolic meaning of "The Song of Wandering Aengus" in terms of its allusions and its symbols. How do the setting and the mood support the symbolic meaning of the poem? What do you think the last two lines mean?

3. **Comparing.** Both "The Secret Heart" and "The Song of Wandering Aengus" reflect a state of mind that is somewhere between memory and dream. The child in the first poem lies "half in dreams" when he sees an image that stays with him forever. The speaker in the second poem experiences a dreamlike vision that he, too, always remembers. Find several similarities and differences in the ways the two poems treat the idea of an impression or experience that stays with a person forever.

4. **Analyzing Rhyme and Meter.** Notice that "The Secret Heart" is written in rhyming couplets. How does that structure affect the sound of the poem? Analyze the meter of the poem. Review Chapter 1 to identify the various kinds of meter. The poem has a regular meter, but it does occasionally vary. What effect do the variations have on the poem?

Writing About Literature

Several suggestions for writing projects are given below. You may be asked to complete one or more of these projects. If you have any questions about how to begin a writing assignment, review Using the Writing Process, beginning on page 219.

1. **Describing a Dream or a Memory.** Think of a dream or a memory that has had a lasting effect on you. Write down the sequence of events in that dream or memory. List any colors, objects, actions, or key details that you remember. Using strong images and clear language, describe your dream or memory and explain any symbolic meaning it has for you.

2. **Analyzing the Symbolism of a Poem.** In the lesson you studied some ways in which Coffin and Yeats used symbolism in their poems. On the basis of what you learned, analyze the symbolism in one of the poems from a previous chapter. Reread the poem several times. Think about its images,

metaphors, and allusions. Listen to the sounds of the poem. Look closely at the details and the action of the poem. As you note each element, think about whether it has any symbolic meaning. Then write several paragraphs that show how the poet develops the symbolism in the poem.

3. **Creating a Setting.** Create an imaginary setting you might like to go to. It can be strange and magical, or it can be realistic. Write a description of the place, giving details, colors, actions, and events, as Yeats does in "The Song of Wandering Aengus." You do not need to include any symbolic meaning. Concentrate instead on communicating your feelings about the setting and your reasons for wanting to go there.

Interpreting Poetry

*I*n the first two units you learned some important skills needed to understand poetry. Unit One taught you how to listen to the sounds of poems, and Unit Two taught you how to identify the images that poets create. In this unit you will learn how to interpret a poem. Interpretation involves examining the elements of a poem, both individually and in combination, to gain a comprehensive understanding of the poem.

When you read books, listen to music, or look at a painting, you gain information and knowledge. Good art is revealing. It gives you new ideas or suggests new ways of perceiving old ideas. Often, good art provides an insight into some aspect of the world, your culture, or your own life.

You may read poems for many reasons, but primarily you read poems in order to understand what a poet has to say. As you have already learned, poets write about diverse subjects. When you understand a poem, you share for a moment the poet's vision, feelings, and perceptions.

Each of the chapters in Unit Three introduces you to one or more elements of a poem that help you to interpret its meaning. In Chapter 7, for example, you will examine the speaker, or the voice that talks in a poem. Knowing who the speaker is, analyzing the speaker's personality, and discovering the speaker's views about life are essential to understanding any poem. In Chapter 8 you will study the structure of poetry and learn how a poem's design affects its meaning. In Chapter 9 you will read one of the best-known poems in English, John Donne's "A Valediction: Forbidding Mourning," and use the skills you have studied to interpret the poem.

Chapter 7

Selections

Invitation Standing
PAUL BLACKBURN

I Heard a Fly Buzz
EMILY DICKINSON

Birches
ROBERT FROST

Lesson

Meaning and the Speaker

About the Selections

Nature plays an important role in your life. It is part of your physical environment, as well as a force that stirs your emotions and imagination. Just as nature may inspire certain feelings in you, it has been a source of inspiration for artists of every kind, from composers to painters to poets.

Like all artists, poets must look both inside and outside themselves. They must observe the natural world around them, and study the internal world of feelings, moods, and thoughts. Poets often use images from nature—its vastness and splendor, its cycles of death and rebirth, its mystery and complexity—to explore their own inner feelings.

In each of the poems that you are about to read, an object in nature plays a significant role. In "Invitation Standing" Paul Blackburn creates a vivid picture of springtime through the central image of a leaf. The fly in Emily Dickinson's "I Heard a Fly Buzz" intrudes into a sorrowful deathbed scene and, for a moment, becomes the focus of a dying person's attention. The speaker in "Birches" creates several images of trees bending to the ground with their burdens of snow, ice, or climbing boys.

Paul Blackburn was born in St. Albans, Vermont, in 1926. He was educated at New York University and the University of Wisconsin. While Blackburn was in college, he began writing poems. He had little success getting them published. Blackburn's poetry eventually came to the attention of the influential American poet Ezra Pound. Pound encouraged the young man and introduced him to other poets, who also praised his work. In 1955 Blackburn's first book, *The Dissolving Fabric,* was published.

Until his death in 1971, Blackburn spent most of his adult life in France, where he lectured at the University of Toulouse. He is respected for his own poetry and for his many excellent translations of medieval French literature.

Emily Dickinson (1839–1886), author of "I Heard a Fly Buzz," was born in Amherst, Massachusetts. Except for a year at college, she spent her life in Amherst. Dickinson continued her adult life in the house where she was brought up, and as she grew older, she rarely left the house or its garden.

Emily Dickinson was a very private poet. She wrote more than 1,700 poems, yet she wanted none of them to be published. A few friends were occasionally allowed glimpses of selected poems, but the majority of her work was not read until after her death.

Dickinson's poems are brief, and her style is plain and spare. Yet even though her world was enclosed and her breadth of experience limited, Dickinson used her poetry to explore questions about faith, love, death, and nature. As you will see when you read "I Heard a Fly Buzz," Dickinson's work is filled with concise, effective imagery that is heightened by her contained style. Today literary critics consider her to be one of America's greatest poets.

Robert Frost was born in San Francisco in 1884, but his family moved to Massachusetts when he was still a child. After leaving college, Frost bought a farm in New Hampshire. The farming venture failed, however, and he moved to England in 1912. There he published his first two books of poetry. The second collection, *North of Boston,* was well received in the United States. By the time he returned to the United States, he had established a reputation for sophisticated poetry crafted within traditional verse forms. After his return to New Hampshire, Frost continued to write until his death in 1963.

Many readers feel that Robert Frost's poetry is much easier to read and understand than the work of other modern poets. Although many of his poems, like "Birches," are more complicated than they appear, his simple language and rural subject matter make the poems very accessible to readers.

Lesson Preview

The lesson that follows the three poems focuses on the importance of the speaker in each poem. In order to understand the meaning of a poem, you need to identify who is speaking.

The questions that follow will help you identify the speakers and their roles in the poems in this chapter. As you read, think about how you would answer these questions.

1 In "Invitation Standing" who or what is the speaker?

2 In "I Heard a Fly Buzz" what is unusual about the speaker's situation? What feelings does the speaker express?

3 What do you learn about the speaker in "Birches"?

4 What theme do you think the speaker in "Birches" is expressing?

Vocabulary

Here are some difficult words that appear in the poems that follow. Study the words and their definitions, as well as the sentences that show how the words are used. This will help you get the most from your reading.

heaves rhythmical rising motions. *The heaves of the waves during the storm made everyone on the cruise ship seasick.*

keepsakes things that are kept in memory of an event; mementos. *At the dance, each couple was presented with an engraved keepsake as a memento of the evening.*

crazes produces tiny cracks in the glaze. *One dishonest craftsman crazes the glaze on his pottery so that customers will think he sells antiques.*

bracken large, coarse ferns. *The forest bracken was so thick that it had choked out some of the small trees.*

poise balance. *The performer lost her poise on the tightrope and fell into the safety net below.*

Invitation Standing

PAUL BLACKBURN

Bring a leaf to me
just a leaf just a
spring leaf, an
april leaf
5 just
      come

Blue sky
never mind
Spring rain
10 never mind
Reach up and
take a leaf and
      come
just come

I Heard a Fly Buzz

EMILY DICKINSON

I heard a Fly buzz—when I died—
The Stillness in the Room
Was like the Stillness in the Air—
Between the Heaves of Storm—

5 The Eyes around—had wrung them dry—
   And Breaths were gathering firm
   For that last Onset—when the King
   Be witnessed—in the Room—

   I willed my Keepsakes—Signed away
10 What portion of me be
   Assignable—and then it was
   There interposed a Fly—

   With Blue—uncertain stumbling Buzz—
   Between the light—and me—
15 And then the Windows failed—and then
   I could not see to see—

Birches

ROBERT FROST

When I see birches bend to left and right
Across the lines of straighter darker trees,
I like to think some boy's been swinging them.
But swinging doesn't bend them down to stay
5 As ice storms do. Often you must have seen them
Loaded with ice a sunny winter morning
After a rain. They click upon themselves
As the breeze rises, and turn many-colored
As the stir cracks and crazes their enamel.
10 Soon the sun's warmth makes them shed crystal shells
Shattering and avalanching on the snow crust—
Such heaps of broken glass to sweep away

You'd think the inner dome of heaven had fallen.
They are dragged to the withered bracken by the load,
15 And they seem not to break; though once they are bowed
So low for long, they never right themselves:
You may see their trunks arching in the woods
Years afterwards, trailing their leaves on the ground
Like girls on hands and knees that throw their hair
20 Before them over their heads to dry in the sun.
But I was going to say when Truth broke in
With all her matter of fact about the ice storm,
I should prefer to have some boy bend them
As he went out and in to fetch the cows—
25 Some boy too far from town to learn baseball,
Whose only play was what he found himself,
Summer or winter, and could play alone.
One by one he subdued his father's trees
By riding them down over and over again
30 Until he took the stiffness out of them,
And not one but hung limp, not one was left
For him to conquer. He learned all there was
To learn about not launching out too soon
And so not carrying the tree away
35 Clear to the ground. He always kept his poise
To the top branches, climbing carefully
With the same pains you use to fill a cup
Up to the brim, and even above the brim.
Then he flung outward, feet first, with a swish,
40 Kicking his way down through the air to the ground.
So was I once myself a swinger of birches.
And so I dream of going back to be.
It's when I'm weary of considerations,
And life is too much like a pathless wood
45 Where your face burns and tickles with the cobwebs

Broken across it, and one eye is weeping
From a twig's having lashed across it open.
I'd like to get away from earth awhile
And then come back to it and begin over.
50   May no fate willfully misunderstand me
And half grant what I wish and snatch me away
Not to return. Earth's the right place for love:
I don't know where it's likely to go better.
I'd like to go by climbing a birch tree,
55   And climb black branches up a snow-white trunk
Toward heaven, till the tree could bear no more,
But dipped its top and set me down again.
That would be good both going and coming back.
One could do worse than be a swinger of birches.

Reviewing the Selections

Answer each of the following questions. You may look back at the poems if necessary.

Recalling Facts

1. In "Birches" the speaker imagines that the birches are
   - ☐ a. forest spirits.
   - ☐ b. thousands of years old.
   - ☐ c. bent because some boy has been swinging on them.
   - ☐ d. broken because of an ice storm.

Understanding Main Ideas

2. In "Invitation Standing" the speaker wants
   - ☐ a. someone to come visit him.
   - ☐ b. spring to come quickly.
   - ☐ c. a leaf to add to his collection.
   - ☐ d. visitors to chase away his loneliness.

Placing Events in Order

3. In "I Heard a Fly Buzz" the speaker hears the fly
   - ☐ a. just before a storm breaks.
   - ☐ b. before the King enters the room.
   - ☐ c. just after she makes her will.
   - ☐ d. after she passes through the gates of heaven.

Finding Supporting Details

4. In "Birches" what happens when the breeze comes up and the sun rises?
   - ☐ a. The boy begins to swing on trees again.
   - ☐ b. The ice on the trees cracks and falls.
   - ☐ c. The speaker dies and goes to heaven.
   - ☐ d. Truth breaks in with matter-of-fact news.

5. "—and then it was / There <u>interposed</u> a Fly." In this context *interposed* means

□ a. danced.

□ b. exited.

□ c. moved.

□ d. came between.

Interpreting the Selections

Answer each of the following questions. You may look back at the poems if necessary.

6. In "Invitation Standing" the speaker appears to be addressing another person. What can you infer about the speaker's feelings toward that person?

□ a. He likes the person very much.

□ b. He dislikes the person.

□ c. He has no feelings about the person.

□ d. He rarely thinks about the other person.

7. In "I Heard a Fly Buzz" the speaker's attitude toward death seems to be that it

□ a. causes people to behave in strange ways.

□ b. is final.

□ c. should be celebrated as a natural event.

□ d. is an ordinary event.

Finding the
Author's Purpose

8. When Robert Frost observes nature, he discovers parallels to human life. In "Birches" he compares climbing a tree to experiencing
   □ a. life's sadness and pain.
   □ b. life's mysteries.
   □ c. life's challenges.
   □ d. the narrow path to success.

Comparing

9. Compared to the speaker in "Invitation Standing," the speaker in "I Heard a Fly Buzz" is
   □ a. angry.
   □ b. condescending.
   □ c. objective.
   □ d. excited.

Drawing
Conclusions

10. What conclusion can you draw about the speaker in "Birches"?
    □ a. He is a wealthy, successful man.
    □ b. He is growing old.
    □ c. He lives in a town or a city.
    □ d. He is severely depressed.

Meaning and
the Speaker

As you have learned, a speaker is the voice that talks in a poem. Identifying who the speaker is helps you to understand the poem. In autobiographical poems, the speaker's voice may be very similar to the poet's, but often the speaker is a separate character—a person, an animal, or an object—that the poet has invented. Poets have created speakers ranging from rivers and mountains to old cars and deserted barns. Sometimes a poem has more than one speaker, or it includes dialogue—the actual conversation between the characters.

A male poet may not necessarily create a male speaker, just as a female poet may not always create a female speaker. When discussing a speaker, it is often convenient to refer to that speaker as *he* or *she*. Remember, however, that those pronouns do not really identify the sex of the speaker.

When you read a poem, ask yourself, Who is speaking? What do I learn about the speaker's personality from his or her words? In this lesson you will identify the speaker in each poem and study how that voice communicates the poet's message.

Speaker and Audience

"Invitation Standing" is a very short poem and it focuses on one important image—a single leaf in spring. The speaker in the poem is probably someone who appreciates the details of the natural world. The speaker also has his, or her, attention focused on another character—the character whom he asks to come and bring the leaf.

The person, animal, or thing that a speaker addresses is called the audience. Sometimes you are the audience. At other times the audience is a particular person, group, or thing.

1. To whom does the speaker in "Invitation Standing" appear to be talking?

Speaker and Tone

The speaker affects a poem's tone. <u>Tone</u> is a poet's attitude toward his or her subject, audience, or self. A poem may have a formal or an informal tone, or the tone may be gentle, angry, solemn, or playful. The tone of a poem can change; for example, it may develop from worry and concern to relief. Listen carefully for the speaker's tone, for it may be different from the poet's.

The speaker's tone in "Invitation Standing" is gentle and affectionate. Yet at the same time the speaker's tone is urgent. Notice how the speaker asks someone to bring a leaf, then specifies the kind of leaf, then insists "just / come."

The title of "Invitation Standing" contrasts with the speaker's urgent tone. A "standing invitation" refers to an unpressured welcome that one friend gives to another: "Come whenever you want." In Blackburn's poem the standing invitation may imply a perpetual urgency, a constant need to share that friendship.

2. What does the tone reveal about the speaker's state of mind?

"I Heard a Fly Buzz": Reading for Meaning

In "I Heard a Fly Buzz" Emily Dickinson has created a character distinct from herself. The first line of the poem informs you that the speaker is dead: "I heard a Fly buzz—when I died."

In the poem the speaker experiences the last few moments before death with extraordinary calmness and objectivity. She notes the ominous "Stillness in the Room." She sees the faces of the people around her, their eyes wrung dry from crying, and she hears the people holding their breaths in anticipation of death. The speaker finishes making her will.

A moment before death, a noisy fly intrudes into the room. The speaker becomes aware of the fly. "With Blue—uncertain stumbling Buzz," it blocks her line of vision. The fly is the last thing she sees, for then she dies.

What is unusual about the poem is the way in which the speaker describes her own death. The scene is re-created as a flashback. A <u>flashback</u> is a scene, a conversation, or an event that interrupts the present action to show something that happened in the past. Line 1, "I heard a Fly buzz—when I died—," is the present action of the poem. The remainder of the poem is a flashback. In it the speaker details the atmosphere and events preceding her death.

3. Write several adjectives that describe the speaker's attitude toward experiencing death. What is your response to her way of describing that scene?

The Speaker's Personality

In "I Heard a Fly Buzz" Emily Dickinson reveals more about the personality of the speaker than Paul Blackburn does in his poem. The personality of Dickinson's speaker is shown through the speaker's own words and actions.

The speaker's words reveal her observations about her deathbed scene. For example, she is sensitive to the atmosphere in the room and to the grief of the people around her. Yet she does not go into detail about her surroundings. She recounts the scene in a surprisingly impersonal way. Everyone, including herself, is resigned to the certainty of her death.

She wills away "What portion of me be / Assignable." The speaker's action implies that her worldly goods are her assignable portion; her body and soul are willed to no one. Detached and independent, she is prepared for death.

4. What kind of person do you think the speaker was in life?

5. Do you think the fly might be a symbol for something else?

"Birches": Reading for Meaning

The speaker in Robert Frost's poem "Birches" is thinking about the birch trees in the forest that stand bowed, rather than straight like other trees. His thoughts are divided into several distinct sections. In the opening lines he introduces the image of a boy swinging on the birches, bending them to the ground with his weight. Then in line 5 he digresses, or wanders from the main point. In his long digression (lines 5 through 20), the speaker describes how the birches are affected by ice storms. In line 21 the speaker returns to his original image, developing the picture of a boy swinging on the birches. The speaker includes himself in the poem in line 41: "So was I once myself a swinger of birches." From that line until the end of the poem, he reveals his own feelings and ideas about the connection between birches and life.

6. While describing the birches and his feelings about them, the speaker tells you about himself. What do you learn about the speaker in the poem? His background? His present circumstances? His outlook on life? His personality?

Symbols in "Birches"

Frost develops the image of the birches into a symbol. Remember that a symbol is a person, a place, or an object that stands for something other or more important than itself.

In the poem you see a boy living in the country who has few ways to amuse himself; his "only play" is to climb birch trees. "One by one he subdued his father's trees," until "not one was left / For him to conquer." The trees become a symbol for the tests and challenges of childhood. Climbing the birches becomes a symbol of the process by which children learn to approach adulthood.

7. Reread lines 32 through 38. What does the poet mean when he says, "He learned all there was / To learn about not launching out too soon"? Identify both the surface meaning and the symbolic meaning.

8. What is symbolized by the boy's climbing carefully and keeping his poise?

Speaker and Theme

Frost reveals his theme, or underlying message, through the speaker and the symbols of the poem. The theme is different from the subject of the poem. Theme is the poet's insight or comment about the human condition.

In most poems the theme is implied, or suggested, rather than stated directly. To find the theme, you need to read the poem carefully, looking for evidence of what the poet is saying about life. In "Birches" the theme emerges from the images and the symbols of a boy playing in the trees and from the speaker's thoughts.

In the poem the boy learns from the trees by "riding them down over and over again." The speaker, an older man, dreams of climbing birch trees again in order "to get away from earth awhile." For the speaker, birches symbolize a release from the "pathless wood" of adult life. Yet climbing birches does not represent an escape, but a rest for one "weary of considerations."

Although the speaker dreams of breaking away from his present life, he does not want to leave permanently. In spite of life's complexities he feels it is better to be part of life than to escape from it.

9. How does the speaker's personality reinforce the theme of the poem?

Questions for Thought and Discussion

The questions and activities that follow will help you to explore the poems in this chapter in more depth and at the same time develop your critical thinking skills.

1. **Comparing.** Compare the speakers in "I Heard a Fly Buzz" and "Birches." How are they similar? How are they different?

2. **Identifying Tone.** How would you describe the speaker's tone in "Birches"? How does it change during the course of the poem?

3. **Analyzing Figurative Language.** Robert Frost uses several figures of speech in "Birches." Find at least one example each of a metaphor, a simile, and personification. In each case explain how the figure of speech gives you a new way of looking at one of the things.

Writing About Literature

Several suggestions for writing projects are given below. You may be asked to complete one or more of these projects. If you have any questions about how to begin a writing assignment, review Using the Writing Process, beginning on page 219.

1. **Composing a Poem.** Reread "Invitation Standing." Using Paul Blackburn's poem as a model, write your own poetic "invitation" to a friend. Include any image that you think will sound inviting. Think about your poem's tone.

2. **Describing a Scene.** Think of an event that is or will be important in your life. Then imagine an insignificant incident or object that you notice at the same time as that event. Bring the two elements together in a poem or a paragraph. Use Emily Dickinson's poem as a model.

3. **Analyzing Devices of Sound.** Review the information in Chapter 2 about alliteration and assonance. Choose ten lines in "Birches" and identify the patterns of alliteration and assonance. Write one or two paragraphs explaining the effect those devices of sound have on the poem's mood and tone.

Chapter 8

Selections

I Am the Only Being
EMILY BRONTË

Excerpts from *Song of Myself*
WALT WHITMAN

Heart Crown and Mirror
GUILLAUME APOLLINAIRE

Lesson

Structure and Meaning

About the Selections

Poems can vary in size, shape, and form, but they can usually be divided into two main groups, or types, of poems: narrative and lyric. A <u>narrative poem</u> tells a true or imagined story. The story may be brief, with just one character, or it may be long, with several characters and a complicated plot. A <u>lyric poem</u> is a poem that has a single speaker and expresses a deeply felt thought or emotion. The speaker does not have a specific audience; that is, the speaker seems to be addressing himself or herself.

Just as you find variety in the genres of poems, so you also find variety in the forms in which poems are presented. Some poems are written in a fixed form, such as the sonnet and the haiku. The lines and stanzas in certain poems may follow regular patterns, but in other poems both the lines and stanzas may vary their patterns. In this chapter you will read three poems that differ in form and meaning.

Emily Brontë, who wrote "I Am the Only Being," was one of three remarkable sisters, Charlotte, Emily, and Anne, who all published novels that became classics of English literature. Emily was born in 1818 in Yorkshire, England. Her father was a minister in a small, bleak parish on the Yorkshire moors.

The Brontës were a close family. The children had few contacts with the world outside the parsonage, so they spent a great deal of time together. The sisters invented stories and poems that their brother Branwell, an artist, illustrated.

When Emily was about nineteen years old, she taught briefly at a boarding school. Little is known about her life away from home, but from references in her own writings and in those of her family, she may have fallen in love. After a year away, she returned home and remained there for the rest of her life.

Emily Brontë composed many of her poems, including "I Am the Only Being," when she was in her teens and early twenties. In 1847 she published *Wuthering Heights,* her only novel. Although it was not well received when it first appeared, it has since become one of the most famous novels in English literature. A year after its publication, Emily died of tuberculosis.

Walt Whitman, the author of "Song of Myself," was born on Long Island, New York, in 1819 and grew up in Brooklyn. A printer and a journalist, Whitman began to write stories and poems for the newspapers he edited. In 1855 Whitman printed a small book of his own poetry called *Leaves of Grass.* "Song of Myself" was the first poem in the book. During the next thirty-seven years he periodically reprinted the volume, each time adding more poems. By the time Whitman died in 1892 the book had been revised nine times.

Leaves of Grass was unlike any other poetry being published in Whitman's era, and it created a great deal of controversy. The poems celebrated the relationship between humanity and nature; they often dwelt on the beauty of the United States and of its ideals. Composed in free verse, the poems were often very long. Sometimes the speaker was joyful, and sometimes he was angrily insistent. Despite the complaints the work initially raised, *Leaves of Grass* greatly influenced many nineteenth- and twentieth-century poets.

Guillaume Apollinaire (1880–1918), author of "Heart Crown and Mirror," was an Italian-born French poet and critic. A leading figure in the Paris art world in the years prior to World War I, Apollinaire experimented with radical new forms of poetry. A friend of Pablo Picasso, Apollinaire supported visual experimentation, and he transferred some of Picasso's ideas about painting to his own poems.

Apollinaire manipulated type on the page so that letters and words produced pictures, extending the written meaning of poetry into the realm of visual art. In addition to these poems, he wrote plays and short stories. Apollinaire's literary and artistic experiments influenced many twentieth-century poets and artists.

Lesson Preview

The lesson that follows the three poems focuses on their structure—the poet's arrangement or overall design of the poem. Structure refers to the way the words and lines are arranged to produce a particular effect. The poems in this chapter offer three contrasting structures, each supporting the poet's subject and meaning.

The questions that follow will help you to understand the structure of each poem and analyze the relationship between structure and meaning in a poem. As you read, think about how you would answer these questions.

1 In Emily Brontë's poem "I Am the Only Being," how are the speaker's thoughts organized? How do they develop from one stanza to the next?

2 How does the structure and organization of "Song of Myself" differ from "I Am the Only Being"?

3 What is Whitman's attitude toward the world? Himself? Nature? Other people?

4 How does the shape of each of the poems in "Heart Crown and Mirror" contribute to its meaning?

Vocabulary

Here are some difficult words that appear in the poems that follow. Study the words and their definitions, as well as the sentences that show how the words are used. This will help you get the most from your reading.

natal relating to one's birth. *Doctors who specialize in natal medicine frequently care for premature infants.*

drear dreary; melancholy. *Since the rainy weather was so dim and drear, we preferred to stay indoors by the bright fire.*

servile cringingly submissive. *We were annoyed by the servile waiter who was constantly refolding our napkins and hovering over our table.*

distillation the process of heating and then condensing a mixture to produce a pure substance. *The distillation of polluted water helps to purify it.*

belched to erupt or explode violently. *The erupting volcano belched forth lava and ash.*

eddies currents of air or water moving against the main current in a circular motion. *In the gentle eddies of the brook, we could see tiny fish swirling with the current.*

trill a wavering or trembling sound made by singing or playing two notes rapidly back and forth. *Several composers have written pieces in which the flute's trill sounds like a bird.*

specters ghosts; phantoms. *In the guilty man's nightmare, the specters of his victims came back to haunt him.*

I Am the Only Being

EMILY BRONTË

I am the only being whose doom
No tongue would ask, no eye would mourn;
I never caused a thought of gloom,
A smile of joy, since I was born.

5   In secret pleasure, secret tears,
This changeful life has slipped away,
As friendless after eighteen years,
As lone as on my natal day.

There have been times I cannot hide,
10 There have been times when this was drear,
When my sad soul forgot its pride
And longed for one to love me here.

But those were in the early glow
Of feelings since subdued by care;
15 And they have died so long ago,
I hardly now believe they were.

First melted off the hope of youth,
Then fancy's rainbow fast withdrew;
And then experience told me truth
20 In mortal bosoms never grew.

'Twas grief enough to think mankind
All hollow, servile, insincere;
But worse to trust to my own mind
And find the same corruption there.

Structure and Meaning

Excerpts from

Song of Myself

WALT WHITMAN

[1]
I celebrate myself,
And what I assume you shall assume,
For every atom belonging to me as good belongs to you.

I loafe and invite my soul,
5   I lean and loafe at my ease . . . . observing a spear of summer grass.

[2]
Houses and rooms are full of perfumes . . . . the shelves are crowded
    with perfumes,
I breathe the fragrance myself, and know it and like it,
The distillation would intoxicate me also, but I shall not let it.

The atmosphere is not a perfume . . . . it has no taste of the
    distillation . . . . it is odorless,
10   It is for my mouth forever . . . . I am in love with it,
I will go to the bank by the wood and become undisguised and naked,
I am mad for it to be in contact with me.

The smoke of my own breath,
Echoes, ripples, and buzzed whispers . . . . loveroot, silkthread,
    crotch and vine,
15   My respiration and inspiration . . . . the beating of my heart . . . .
    the passing of blood and air through my lungs,
The sniff of green leaves and dry leaves, and of the shore and
    darkcolored sea-rocks, and of hay in the barn,

The sound of the belched words of my voice . . . . words loosed to
    the eddies of the wind,
A few light kisses . . . . a few embraces . . . . a reaching around of arms,
The play of shine and shade on the trees as the supple boughs wag,
20   The delight alone or in the rush of the streets, or along the fields
    and hillsides,
The feeling of health . . . . the full-noon trill . . . . the song of me
    rising from bed and meeting the sun.

Have you reckoned a thousand acres much? Have you reckoned the
    earth much?
Have you practiced so long to learn to read?
Have you felt so proud to get at the meaning of poems?

25   Stop this day and night with me and you shall possess the origin of
    all poems,
You shall possess the good of the earth and sun . . . . there are millions
    of suns left,
You shall no longer take things at second or third hand . . . . nor look
    through the eyes of the dead . . . . nor feed on the specters in
    books,
You shall not look through my eyes either, nor take things from me,
You shall listen to all sides and filter them from yourself.

*[Sections 3 through 51, from line 30 to line 1320, are omitted. In those forty-nine
sections, Whitman celebrates all aspects of life: grass, people alive and dead, birth,
death, a country barn, a clipper ship, marriage, a runaway slave, war, earth, the
sea, space, time, and so on. Section 52, which begins at line 1321, is the last section
of the poem.]*

[52]
The spotted hawk swoops by and accuses me . . . . he complains of
    my gab and my loitering.

I too am not a bit tamed . . . . I too am untranslatable,
I sound my barbaric yawp over the roofs of the world.

The last scud of day holds back for me,
1325 It flings my likeness after the rest and true as any on the shadowed
          wilds,
It coaxes me to the vapor and the dusk.

I depart as air . . . . I shake my white locks at the runaway sun,
I effuse my flesh in eddies and drift it in lacy jags.

I bequeath myself to the dirt to grow from the grass I love,
1330 If you want me again look for me under your bootsoles.

You will hardly know who I am or what I mean,
But I shall be good health to you nevertheless,
And filter and fiber your blood.

Failing to fetch me at first keep encouraged,
1335 Missing me one place search another,
I stop some where waiting for you

Heart Crown and Mirror

Guillaume Apollinaire

Translated by Kenneth Koch

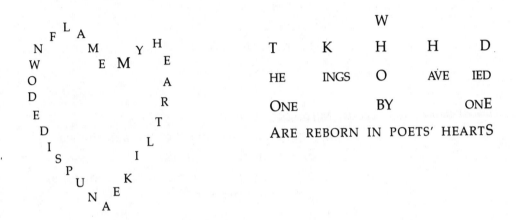

```
            IN    THIS
        IONS      MIR
      FLECT        ROR
       RE           I
      THE           AM
     LIKE  Guillaume  EN
     NOT          CLOSED
     AND  Apollinaire  A
      GELS         LIVE
       AN          AND
      GINE        REAL
       MA         AS
        I    YOU
```

Reviewing the Selections

Answer each of the following questions. You may look back at the poems if necessary.

Recalling Facts

1. How old is the speaker in "I Am the Only Being"?
   - ☐ a. twelve
   - ☐ b. eighteen
   - ☐ c. twenty-one
   - ☐ d. thirty-seven

Understanding Main Ideas

2. In "Mirror" the poet is
   - ☐ a. urging people to look beyond appearances.
   - ☐ b. describing his own death.
   - ☐ c. explaining how a mirror shows good and evil in human beings.
   - ☐ d. pretending to be an angel.

Placing Events in Order

3. In "Song of Myself" the spotted hawk complains to the speaker about his "gab"
   - ☐ a. at the beginning of the poem.
   - ☐ b. right after the speaker mentions the "sound of the belched words of my voice."
   - ☐ c. before the speaker describes the taste of the atmosphere.
   - ☐ d. before the speaker says, "I shake my white locks."

Finding Supporting Details

4. In "Heart Crown and Mirror" each poem
   - ☐ a. has the shape of its subject.
   - ☐ b. tells something about love.
   - ☐ c. can be read clockwise and counterclockwise.
   - ☐ d. has more than one shape.

5. "The play of shine and shade on the trees
   as the <u>supple</u> boughs wag. . . ." In this context
   supple means
   - ☐ a. thick.
   - ☐ b. stiff.
   - ☐ c. flexible.
   - ☐ d. green.

Interpreting the Selections

Answer each of the following questions. You may look back at the poems if necessary.

6. In "I Am the Only Being" the speaker is
   - ☐ a. determined to find love again.
   - ☐ b. disgusted with life and with herself.
   - ☐ c. unsure about whether or not she
         wants friends.
   - ☐ d. happy that she has subdued her feelings.

7. In "Song of Myself" the poet views his audience as
   - ☐ a. equal to himself in every way.
   - ☐ b. intellectually inferior to himself.
   - ☐ c. honest but naive.
   - ☐ d. corrupt beyond redemption.

8. In "Heart Crown and Mirror" Guillaume
   Apollinaire wants to show that
   ☐ a. life imitates art.
   ☐ b. a poem does not need to rhyme.
   ☐ c. a poem can have a visual impact.
   ☐ d. poets are artists, too.

Comparing

9. The poems by Emily Brontë and Walt Whitman
   differ greatly in their attitude toward life. Which
   pair of adjectives best characterizes the difference
   between the two poems?
   ☐ a. concerned—whimsical
   ☐ b. bitter—joyful
   ☐ c. open-minded—uncritical
   ☐ d. serene—anxious

Drawing
Conclusions

10. After reading several sections of "Song of
    Myself," what conclusion can you draw about
    the speaker?
    ☐ a. He is shy and self-effacing.
    ☐ b. He is thoughtless and lazy.
    ☐ c. He is kind and courteous.
    ☐ d. He is curious and confident.

Structure and Meaning

As you learned in the Lesson Preview, the structure of a poem refers to the poet's arrangement or overall design of a poem. Line length is one component of structure. In earlier chapters you read poems with a variety of line lengths. Each line in William Carlos Williams's poem "The Locust Tree in Flower," for example, contains just one word. Some of Dylan Thomas's lines in "Fern Hill" are very long. In this chapter many of Walt Whitman's lines in "Song of Myself" are as long as prose sentences. Each poet you have studied has deliberately used line length to reflect his or her feelings about a subject.

In addition to controlling line length, a poet creates structure by grouping lines together to develop thoughts and ideas. By grouping lines, he or she builds a framework to connect the parts that form the complete poem. In this lesson you will examine the structure of several poems and study the relationship between a poem's structure and its meaning.

"I Am the Only Being": Reading for Meaning

Emily Brontë's poem concerns a person who is lonely and unhappy. In stanza 1 the speaker says that she has never caused either joy or sadness, and in stanza 2 she reveals that she has passed her life in "secret pleasure, secret tears." She remains as alone today as at the moment of her birth.

1. Reread stanzas 3 and 4. Why is the speaker so alone now? What character trait does she mention that might explain her loneliness?

The poem reveals the bitterness that loneliness can create. The speaker admits that her solitude makes her sad and that she once longed for someone to love her. But that "early glow" of feeling faded, and with it faded her other generous and hopeful feelings. From the few contacts she has with others, she concludes that "truth / In mortal bosoms never grew;" she finds insincerity and falseness in everyone she meets.

2. What does the speaker mean by "fancy's rainbow" in line 18?

3. What attitude toward the world does the speaker express in the last two stanzas? What conclusions has she made?

"I Am the Only Being" is a sad, bitter poem, made even sadder by the fact that the speaker is only eighteen years old.

Traditional Structure

Emily Brontë's poem is divided into six quatrains, or four-line stanzas. A stanza, as you have learned, is a group of lines that forms a section of a poem. Often the stanzas in a poem have a fixed number of lines and the same rhyme scheme and meter. A poem with a fixed pattern of stanzas is said to have a traditional structure.

4. What is the rhyme scheme of "I Am the Only Being"? How does that rhyme scheme contribute to the unity of each stanza?

In Chapter 1 you learned about both rhyme scheme and meter. Meter, you will recall, is the regular pattern of stressed and unstressed syllables in a line of poetry. The meter of a poem sets up a rhythm, although a poet will sometimes break the rhythm to emphasize a word, an idea, or a sound. To determine the meter of a poem, you scan lines, identifying the number of feet.

5. Scan Emily Brontë's poem and identify the meter. Are all the lines in the poem in the same meter? Explain your answer.

Stanzas help poets organize their ideas. They can be considered units of thought, just as paragraphs are units of thought in prose writing. Reread "I Am the Only Being." Notice that Brontë uses the first stanza to establish her main point: the speaker's loneliness and isolation. That stanza is like the topic statement at the beginning of a prose work.

6. How does Brontë develop her main point in the second stanza?

7. Reread the last stanza. How does it serve as a "concluding paragraph" to the poem? What effect does the last stanza have on you?

Emily Brontë's organization is just one example of the many ways in which poets organize their ideas and thoughts. If you think about the poems you have already studied, you will realize that they have great variations in structure.

"Song of Myself": Reading for Meaning

In "Song of Myself" Walt Whitman expresses a joyous, passionate, exuberant view of life. "Song of Myself" reflects Whitman's belief that everything in the universe is present in everything else. To Whitman, past and present, good and bad, and all living things are connected. In the poem he revels in the wonder of learning and in experiencing everything life has to offer.

In the first line of the poem, the speaker, who mirrors the voice of the poet, celebrates himself. The celebration immediately extends, however, to you, the poem's audience:

> I celebrate myself,
> And what I assume you shall assume,
> For every atom belonging to me as good belongs to you.

The speaker says that he will share his assumptions with all humanity.

In "Song of Myself" the speaker uses his senses to reveal his feelings about the world. In section 2, for example, he smells the perfumes in houses and tastes the air around him.

8. Read section 2 and find examples of how Whitman's speaker appeals to touch, sound, and sight.

The speaker enthusiastically offers you his observations of experience and joy. He not only shares his excitement but also invites you to join him in making your own discoveries: "Stop this day and night with me and you shall possess the origin of all poems."

9. Reread sections 1 and 2. How does the speaker directly involve you in his poem?

In the last section [52] of "Song of Myself," Whitman's speaker says he knows he has been talking too much. A spotted hawk flies by and complains about his "gab," but even then the poet feels a connection with the hawk. He expresses his relationship to the natural world in the metaphor: "I sound my barbaric yawp over the roofs of the world."

10. What does that metaphor mean?

At the end of the poem, the sun is setting: "The last scud of day holds back for me." The image of a setting sun is an implicit metaphor for death.

11. Reread line 1325 to the end of the poem. How does the speaker develop the metaphor of the setting sun?

12. Where does the speaker say you should look if you want to find him again? Why will he be "good health" to you?

Use of Free Verse

Walt Whitman pioneered the use of free verse. At the time he was writing, his lack of meter and a rhyme scheme and his irregular rhythms and line lengths aroused strong criticism. Yet the free verse form, with its openness, spontaneity, and naturalness, is perfectly suited to Whitman's subject and meaning.

Compare the tightly structured stanzas of "I Am the Only Being" to the flowing irregularity of "Song of Myself." The structures of the two poems reflect the differing views of the two speakers.

13. Describe the differences in mood, or general atmosphere, in the two poems. How is the structure of each poem suited to its mood?

Verse Paragraphs. Free verse does *not* mean that a poem has no structure. In free verse the structure evolves from the poet's ideas, images, thoughts, and feelings. The poet controls the structure by grouping words and phrases into lines and organizing lines into distinct units of thought. A verse paragraph is a group of lines in a poem that forms a unit similar to a prose paragraph. A verse paragraph is as long or as short as the content requires. The line lengths within each verse may vary, as they do in "Song of Myself."

14. Choose one verse paragraph in Whitman's poem and explain how it encompasses a distinct unit of thought.

Rhythm. Although free verse lacks both a rhyme scheme and meter, it does contain rhythm, usually the rhythm of natural speech. In "Song of Myself" the rhythm changes according to the poet's mood. Reread the first three lines of the poem and notice the varying line lengths. As the pace of the speaker's thoughts and his emphasis on those thoughts increase, the lines become longer. The opening lines, therefore, suggest the patterns of speech and thoughts of a person becoming excited about his subject.

The following lines also reflect the rhythm of the speaker's thoughts:

I loafe and invite my soul,
I lean and loafe at my ease . . . observing a spear of summer grass.

As the speaker relaxes, he pauses, and then he adds that he is going to watch "a spear of summer grass." The rhythms of free verse encourage the spontaneous addition of new thoughts. The speaker can let his mind wander; he can talk, stop, think, and then complete his thought.

15. What feelings does the spontaneous rhythm create?

Despite the apparent lack of restrictions in free verse, the poet is firmly in control of his work. The form allows the poet to be as expansive as he or she wants to be. However, the poet selects and orders images, details, and ideas just as carefully as a poet using a traditional structure does.

Concrete Poetry

In "I Am the Only Being" the speaker's isolation is reflected and contained by the fixed structure of the poem. The generosity and freedom of "Song of Myself" are conveyed in part through the open, flowing structure of free verse. In both poems the structure reinforces the meanings of the poems.

Some poets have extended the relationship between structure and meaning even further. They have experimented with the way a poem looks on the page by arranging the words and lines of a poem to form a particular, recognizable shape. Concrete poetry conveys meaning through its visual shape on the page. When reading concrete poetry, you absorb a poem's meaning visually, as well as through the words. Concrete poems have been written in the shapes of wings, trees, falling rain, and even the motion of a person swimming laps in a pool.

Guillaume Apollinaire invented a kind of concrete poem that he called a calligramme, a poem in which the arrangement of the typography, or printed letters, helps to present the theme. The shape of a calligramme is determined by its subject. The three calligrammes in this chapter are grouped under the title "Heart Crown and Mirror."

"Heart" is a love poem. The poem is composed of a single simile in which the speaker compares his love to an upside-down flame. A flame suggests warmth, while its upside-down position suggests a heart consumed by love. Even before reading the poem, you can identify the theme by looking at the poem's shape.

16. Reread "Crown." What happens to the kings who have died? How does the shape of the poem help to communicate its meaning?

In "Mirror" the speaker claims to be "enclosed" in a mirror, "alive and real." He suggests that when you look in a mirror you should see the speaker as well as yourself.

17. What does the speaker suggest about viewing the world?

Questions for Thought and Discussion

The questions and activities that follow will help you explore the poems in this chapter in more depth and at the same time develop your critical thinking skills.

1. **Identifying the Speaker.** In "Song of Myself" the speaker sometimes reflects the poet, but at other times the speaker is the "philosophic I"—a person who could be anyone or everyone. Find places in the poem where you think the speaker uses the poet's voice and places where you think the speaker uses a more general voice.

2. **Organizing a Debate.** Organize a debate around the two opinions that follow. One group should support Henry David Thoreau's evaluation of Walt Whitman's poetry. The other group should support the dissenting opinion from *The London Critic.*

> We ought to rejoice greatly in him [Walt Whitman]. He occasionally suggests something a little more than human. . . . Though rude, and sometimes ineffectual, his is a great primitive poem— an alarum [excitement] or trumpet-note ringing through the American camp.   —*Henry David Thoreau*

> Walt Whitman gives us slang in the place of melody, and rowdyism in the place of regularity. . . . Walt Whitman libels the highest type of humanity, and calls his free speech the true utterance of a man; we, who may have been misdirected by civilization, call it the expression of a beast.   —*The London Critic* (1856)

3. **Evaluating.** What are the advantages and disadvantages of concrete poetry such as Guillaume Apollinaire's "Heart Crown and Mirror"?

4. **Comparing.** Review the information about haiku in Chapter 4. How are Guillaume Apollinaire's calligrammes similar to haiku? How are they different?

Writing About Literature

Several suggestions for writing projects follow. You may be asked to complete one or more of these projects. If you have any questions about how to begin a writing assignment, review Using the Writing Process, beginning on page 219.

1. **Experimenting with Form.** Choose a feeling, thought, or event as the subject of a poem. Write a poem of at least one stanza on that subject, using a fixed line length, meter, and rhyme scheme. Then write at least one verse

paragraph in free verse on the same subject. You may want to use the poems by Emily Brontë and Walt Whitman as models for the two kinds of poems.

2. **Analyzing Patterns of Sound.** Choose one or more of the verse paragraphs in "Song of Myself" to read out loud several times. Notice which words are stressed, and listen for other patterns of sound, such as the rising or falling tones of your voice. Then describe the various patterns of sound that you discover and explain how the sounds contribute to the poem's meaning.

3. **Writing a Concrete Poem.** Think of a subject that suggests a feeling or an action, such as happiness, riding a bicycle, or skiing. Decide on an appropriate shape to express that feeling or action. For riding a bicycle, the shape might be a bicycle. Sketch the shape of your poem and then write the words to fit that shape. You could reverse the process by thinking of a shape first and then letting the shape suggest a subject for your concrete poem.

4. **Reporting on Research.** Find out more about Emily Brontë's life. Use at least three sources. In either an oral or a written report, explain whether or not you think Brontë is speaking about herself in "I Am the Only Being."

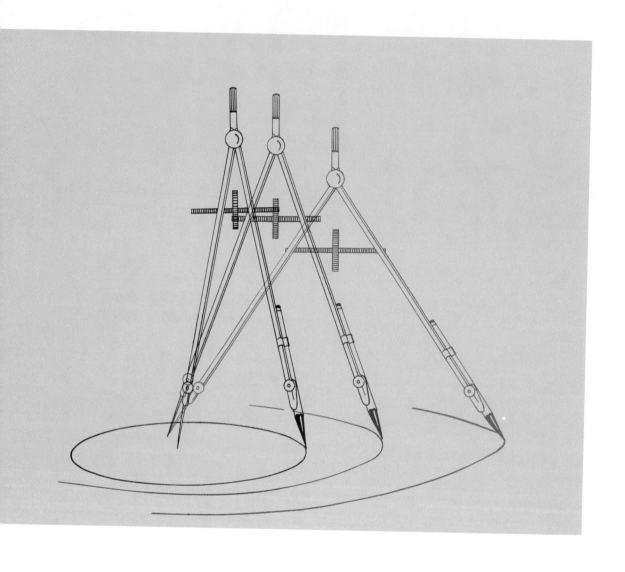

Chapter 9

Selection   *A Valediction: Forbidding Mourning*

JOHN DONNE

Lesson   *Interpreting a Poem*

About the Selection

"A Valediction: Forbidding Mourning" is one of the most famous poems in the English language. It is a complex poem, but one that you can understand if you have some background about how and when it was composed and about how people viewed the world in the early seventeenth century.

The English poet John Donne wrote this work in 1611. Many people believe it was inspired by an event in his own life. Donne was planning an extended trip to France, leaving his wife and children in England. His wife Anne, whom he dearly loved, begged him to stay home. Donne was distressed to see her sadness and may have written "A Valediction: Forbidding Mourning" in an attempt to ease the pain of their separation.

The poem, therefore, is a kind of farewell letter. The word *valediction* means a statement of parting or farewell. According to the title of Donne's poem, the central message of his valediction is that he forbids mourning. In other words, he is urging his beloved not to be sorrowful about his departure. When you read the poem, keep that purpose in mind.

Even though the poem may have been based on Donne's experience, it is more than just a communication between husband and wife. His situation may have inspired the poem, but the poem itself is a celebration of love and an expression of wonder at love's ability to erase time and distance.

One key to reading and understanding "A Valediction: Forbidding Mourning" is knowing how most people in the early 1600s thought about the universe. They viewed the Earth as the center of the universe. Surrounding the Earth, set in spheres that revolved around each other, were the Moon, Sun, stars, and other planets. Beyond those spheres existed the angels and God.

The higher the sphere, the closer it was to God and to purity and perfection. Things that existed below the sphere of the Moon, closest to Earth, were considered *sublunary,* from the Latin word meaning "below the moon." Such things were so distant from God that they were regarded as impure and imperfect. You will notice that Donne uses the word *sublunary* in his poem to make a distinction between earthly love and higher, purer forms of love.

John Donne was born in 1572 into a distinguished English family. His lifetime spanned the reigns of Queen Elizabeth I, King James I, and King Charles I. As a young man, Donne attended Oxford University and studied law in London. A brilliant young man, he was much admired for his poetry. Donne established himself at the court of Queen Elizabeth I and proved to be an able soldier, serving on expeditions with Sir Walter Raleigh and the Earl of Essex. When he was named private secretary to Sir Thomas Egerton, a high official in Elizabeth's court, his future looked very promising.

The picture suddenly changed, however, when he secretly married Anne More in 1601. At the time, most marriages among the nobility and gentry were arranged by the couple's parents. When Sir George More learned of his daughter's secret marriage, he had Donne dismissed from office and imprisoned. Donne was soon released from prison, and he was eventually accepted by his father-in-law. But he never recovered his office at court and spent most of his married life struggling to provide for his family.

In 1615 Donne became a minister in the Church of England. A few years later, he became dean of St. Paul's Cathedral in London, one of the highest positions in the Church of England. In his new position Donne continued to write poetry. Most of his poems and his sermons were published after his death in 1631, and his work has continued to influence many poets.

Lesson Preview

The lesson that follows "A Valediction: Forbidding Mourning" focuses on interpreting a poem. To interpret a poem, you will need to apply all the skills you learned in earlier chapters. You will need to analyze the structure of the poem, recognize the images, and hear the sounds of the language.

The first time you read Donne's poem, you may find it difficult to understand. Use the footnotes and the information you learned about the poet to begin analyzing each stanza. The lesson will study each stanza in detail.

The questions that follow will help you to interpret the poem. As you read, think about how you would answer these questions.

1 Who is the speaker? To whom is he talking?

2 What kind of love is the speaker talking about? How is it different from other kinds of love?

3 To what things does the speaker compare his love?

4 In the last three stanzas what two things are being compared?

Vocabulary

Here are some difficult words that appear in the poem that follows. Study the words and their definitions, as well as the sentences that show how the words are used. This will help you get the most from your reading.

profanation debasement; violation of something holy. *That terrible television series is a profanation of the acting profession.*

laity all the people not included in a given profession. In Donne's poem the word means common, ordinary people. *Although the school was administered by a religious order, it also welcomed students and teachers from the laity.*

trepidation trembling movement; agitation. *When the young actress began to speak, her shaking voice exposed her trepidation.*

breach a breaking apart; rupture. *The violent quarrel created a breach in the relationship of the two old friends.*

hearkens pays attention to; listens to. *The bored class only hearkens to the teacher when he mentions a field trip.*

obliquely indirectly; in a curving manner. *The boomerang flew obliquely, and then curved suddenly to return to its owner.*

just true; perfect; precise. *Since the carpenter's measurements were not just, one of the table legs was longer than the others.*

A Valediction: Forbidding Mourning

John Donne

As virtuous men pass mildly away,[1]
    And whisper to their souls to go,
Whilst some of their sad friends do say,
    "The breath goes now," and some say, "No,"

5 So let us melt,[2] and make no noise,
    No tear-floods, nor sigh-tempests move;
'Twere profanation of our joys
    To tell the laity our love.

Moving of the earth[3] brings harms and fears,
10   Men reckon what it did and meant;
But trepidation of the spheres,
    Though greater far, is innocent.[4]

Dull sublunary lovers' love
    (Whose soul is sense)[5] cannot admit
15 Absence, because it doth remove
    Those things which elemented it.[6]

But we, by a love so much refined
    That our selves know not what it is,
Inter-assured[7] of the mind,
20   Care less, eyes, lips, and hands to miss.

---

1. **pass mildly away:** die. 2. **melt:** part. 3. **moving of the earth:** earthquakes. 4. **innocent:** harmless. The poet suggests that, although the shaking of the heavenly spheres is greater than an earthquake, such a heavenly movement is harmless. 5. **(Whose soul is sense):** whose essence is based on the senses. 6. **which elemented it:** which made up its basic nature. 7. **Inter-assured:** mutually assured.

Our two souls therefore, which are one,
    Though I must go, endure not yet
A breach, but an expansion.
    Like gold to airy thinness beat.

25 If they be two, they are two so
    As stiff twin compasses[8] are two:
Thy soul, the fixed foot, makes no show
    To move, but doth, if the other do;

And though it in the center sit,
30   Yet when the other far doth roam,
It leans, and hearkens after it,
    And grows erect, as that comes home.

Such wilt thou be to me, who must,
    Like the other foot, obliquely run;
35 Thy firmness makes my circle just,
    And makes me end where I begun.

---

8. **stiff twin compasses:** a compass used in drafting, made up of two pointed legs hinged together at one end and used for drawing perfect arcs or circles.

Reviewing the Selection

Answer each of the following questions. You may look back at the poem if necessary.

Recalling Facts

1. According to stanza 6, the speaker is about to
   - ☐ a. die.
   - ☐ b. hunt for gold.
   - ☐ c. leave.
   - ☐ d. kill his beloved.

Understanding Main Ideas

2. The speaker asks his beloved to
   - ☐ a. admit that she really does love him more than anything else in the world.
   - ☐ b. meet him when he returns home.
   - ☐ c. realize that they will be together even though they are separated.
   - ☐ d. remain faithful while he is away.

Placing Events in Order

3. Which of the following images in the poem is presented last?
   - ☐ a. the circle drawn by the compass
   - ☐ b. the death of a virtuous man
   - ☐ c. the gold hammered to thin gold leaf
   - ☐ d. the shaking of the earth

Finding Supporting Details

4. The speaker says that the love he and his beloved share
   - ☐ a. will be destroyed by an earthquake.
   - ☐ b. is dying slowly.
   - ☐ c. is worth more than gold.
   - ☐ d. is not based only on physical passion.

5. "So let us melt, and make no noise, / No tear-floods,
   nor <u>sigh-tempests</u> move." In this context
   sigh-tempests means
   ☐ a. thunderstorms.
   ☐ b. storms of sorrow.
   ☐ c. angry outbursts.
   ☐ d. earthquakes.

Interpreting the Selection

Answer each of the following questions. You may look back at the poem if necessary.

6. From what the speaker reveals in the poem,
   what can you infer about the feelings of the
   woman he loves?
   ☐ a. She is indifferent to him.
   ☐ b. She is in love with another man.
   ☐ c. She loves him as deeply as he loves her.
   ☐ d. She once loved him but no longer does.

7. This poem might best be described as a
   ☐ a. sermon on life and death.
   ☐ b. reasoned argument about the endurance
        of true love.
   ☐ c. complaint against marriage.
   ☐ d. story about traveling.

8. Why does the speaker begin the poem with the
   image of dying men?
   - ☐ a. He is comparing the parting from his
     beloved to death.
   - ☐ b. He feels that the love he has shared with
     his beloved is dying.
   - ☐ c. He wants to show that death is part of life.
   - ☐ d. He wants to show that while he is away he
     will be like a dead man.

9. In stanzas 4 and 5 the speaker compares
   - ☐ a. the soul and the senses.
   - ☐ b. the mind and the body.
   - ☐ c. two souls.
   - ☐ d. two kinds of love.

10. After reading the poem, you can conclude that
    the speaker
    - ☐ a. is secretly glad to be leaving.
    - ☐ b. feels that his absence will be a test
      of his love.
    - ☐ c. wants to comfort his beloved with
      these words.
    - ☐ d. intends to return home soon.

Interpreting a Poem

Some of the poems you have studied in this book are relatively easy to read and understand. Other poems contain more complicated subject matter, imagery, language, or structure. John Donne's "A Valediction: Forbidding Mourning" is probably the most complex poem you have encountered in this book. Like many poems, its meaning is difficult to understand at first. Through careful reading, however, and by using the skills you have already learned, you can analyze the poem and discover its meaning.

In the introduction to this lesson, you read about the circumstances that may have inspired Donne to write "A Valediction: Forbidding Mourning." The poem concerns a man who is leaving his beloved for a time, and who urges her not to mourn their parting. Yet the poem's meaning extends beyond that surface level, and its theme has remained powerful for hundreds of years. In this lesson you will learn how to interpret a poem's meaning.

Analyzing the Structure

In Chapter 8 you learned that the structure of a poem includes not only the arrangement of words into lines and stanzas but also the development of ideas. To understand Donne's poem, you need to understand how he organizes his ideas and connects them from stanza to stanza. A great deal of the poem's power is contained in Donne's organization.

The Statement (Stanzas 1 to 3). In the first three stanzas the poet states his main point: Although we must separate, we need to control our emotions. He states that point through the analogy with which he begins the poem. An <u>analogy</u> is a comparison that demonstrates the similarities between two things. In stanza 1 he creates one half of the analogy: "Virtuous men" die quietly and with dignity. Their passing is so "mild" that even their friends cannot be certain they have actually died. In line 5 Donne completes the analogy: "Like those good men we, too, must separate quietly and with dignity."

1. Reread lines 6 through 8. How does the speaker feel lovers should conduct themselves in parting? What do the following lines mean:

> *'Twere profanation of our joys*
> *To tell the laity our love.*

2. Review the analogy that Donne develops in stanzas 1 and 2. What similarities between the two situations is the speaker emphasizing?

In stanzas 1 and 2 the speaker introduces two ideas. One idea is that the love he shares is *above* ordinary love. Ordinary love is earthly, and therefore imperfect; their love is heavenly, so it is perfect.

The other idea is that the lovers have a choice about how they mourn their separation. They can part with "tear-floods," or they can part quietly. In stanza 3 Donne develops those ideas.

In lines 9 and 10 Donne compares a tearful parting to an earthquake. It will "bring harms and fears," and others will wonder at it. In lines 11 and 12 he compares a quiet, dignified parting to the "trepidation of the spheres," the natural motion of the higher orders of the universe.

3. Reread stanza 3. According to the speaker, how is the "trepidation of the spheres" different from an earthquake? How is the speaker extending the idea of the difference between earthly and heavenly love?

The Argument (Stanzas 4 and 6). In stanza 3 the speaker suggests an argument, or line of reasoning, that he develops in the next three stanzas. The love he shares is special, so separation between the lovers must also be special. They can prove their special love by parting quietly.

In stanzas 4 to 6 he argues why he and his beloved should not mourn.

He explains the differences between commonplace earthly love and their own higher, heavenly love. "Dull sublunary lovers' love" means that earthly love is trapped by the senses. It cannot survive separation because it depends on the lovers' physical presence. If either lover is absent, their love ceases to exist.

4. Reread stanza 5. How is the love that the speaker and his beloved share different from "dull sublunary" love? Find at least two differences.

In stanza 6 the speaker continues his argument. Physical separation signifies nothing because the lovers' two souls are connected. He then introduces a paradox in lines 22 to 24. A <u>paradox</u> is a statement that appears to be self-contradictory or untrue, but which actually reveals a truth. The speaker reasons that although he must leave his beloved, their two souls are not breached, or separated. Instead, they are expanded. The paradox is contained in the statement that the parting, which *is* a separation, will not separate them.

5. What argument does the speaker give to reconcile that contradiction?

The Conceit (Stanzas 7 to 9). The last three stanzas of John Donne's poem complete the valediction by developing a comparison that parallels the lovers' souls and a drafting compass. The comparison is called a <u>conceit</u>—an elaborate and detailed metaphor that compares two very different objects or situations. Although the comparison may seem farfetched, a conceit actually reveals precision, clarity, and logic.

Many seventeenth-century poets, including John Donne, used an intricate, highly intellectual kind of conceit known as a metaphysical conceit. A <u>metaphysical conceit</u> creates parallels between the spiritual qualities of an idea and a physical object. The closing stanzas of "A Valediction: Forbidding Mourning" contain one of the most famous metaphysical conceits in English literature.

Look at the illustration on the next page of a drafting compass. A drafting compass is used for drawing circles and arcs. It consists of two legs hinged at the top. One leg has a pointed tip and is used to fix the center of the circle. The other leg holds a pencil or a pen. By setting the pointed leg firmly on a piece of paper and rotating the other leg, with the pencil touching the paper, around the fixed leg, you can draw a perfect circle. The poet uses the physical object, the compass, as the basis for a metaphysical conceit about the oneness of the two lovers.

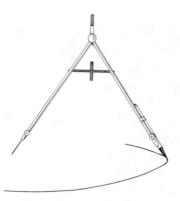

6. Reread stanzas 7 and 8. What part of the compass does each lover represent? Compare the speaker's departure and travels to the movement of the compass.

Images and Figurative Language

John Donne uses images and figurative language to convey his meaning. Appreciating his use of language is important to interpreting the poem.

7. Identify at least three images in the first three stanzas, and explain how each is appropriate to the subject of the poem.

8. Think about the final image of the poem—the circle. What symbolic meaning does a circle have? How is the image of the circle appropriate for the poem?

The poem is filled with figurative language. Although the language is complicated, it helps you discover Donne's deeper levels of meaning.

Notice the implicit metaphor in line 2: "Virtuous men" speak to their souls as though their souls were people.

9. Why do you think the poet uses the word whispers *in that line?*

10. What metaphors occur in line 6? Explain the simile in lines 23 and 24.

The Sounds of the Poem

As you learned in Unit One, what you hear is an essential part of the poem. The meter of "A Valediction: Forbidding Mourning" is sometimes irregular, but the poem has a regular rhyme scheme. Another element of sound in the poem is alliteration, which you read about in Chapter 2. Alliteration adds a musical quality to a poem.

11. What is the dominant meter of the poem? Identify the rhyme scheme.

In "A Valediction: Forbidding Mourning," John Donne has transformed the parting of two lovers into a thoughtful and moving poem about the unchangeable nature of love. Every aspect of the poem—language, sound, images, and structure—contributes to its total meaning.

Questions for Thought and Discussion

The questions and activities that follow will help you explore "A Valediction: Forbidding Mourning" in more depth and at the same time develop your critical thinking skills.

1. **Expressing an Opinion.** In this poem John Donne implies that it is better to remain calm and rational, even in emotionally charged situations. Do you agree with that idea? Why or why not?

2. **Comparing.** Compare Donne's poem to "I Am Not Yours" by Sara Teasdale in Chapter 5. Compare several elements of each poem, such as subject, theme, image, meter, and rhyme. How are they similar? How are they different?

3. **Analyzing Figurative Language.** Review the conceit in the last three stanzas of Donne's poem. What details help you to understand the comparison? What feelings does the conceit suggest? Does the comparison seem appropriate? Why or why not?

Writing About Literature

Several suggestions for writing projects follow. You may be asked to complete one or more of these projects. If you have any questions about how to begin a writing assignment, review Using the Writing Process, beginning on page 219.

1. **Paraphrasing.** Look back at "A Valediction: Forbidding Mourning," and, using what you learned in the lesson, paraphrase the poem. At the end of your restatement, include a paragraph or two in which you comment on the speaker's attitude toward love.

2. **Writing a Letter.** Imagine that the speaker's beloved writes a letter to him after his departure. In it she responds to the arguments he set out in his valediction. Write the kind of letter that you think she might send.

3. **Inventing a Conceit.** Create a conceit that you can develop in prose or in poetry. Remember that a conceit is an extended and elaborate metaphor that compares a deep feeling or a serious thought to a physical object. As Donne did, make your comparison precise, logical, and imaginative. Write several paragraphs or stanzas in which you develop your conceit.

4. **Constructing a Logical Argument.** Imagine that you want to convince a friend to follow a particular course of action. For example, you might want your friend to stop being so shy, to start working harder in school, or to forget some harsh words you once said to him or her. In several paragraphs present a reasoned, logical argument to support your viewpoint. You may want to use figurative language, as Donne did in his poem.

Appreciating
Poetry

*I*n earlier units you studied reading and interpreting poetry. You discovered that part of the pleasure in reading poetry comes from understanding the poet's insights. You probably experienced a sense of accomplishment when you analyzed and combined the individual parts of a poem to discover its meaning.

You may find a poem valuable because of its images, sounds, or themes, as well as for the combination of those elements. That kind of appreciation is common to all good art. When you go to a movie, for example, you may enjoy seeing the complete film. Yet you may also take pleasure in watching certain actors or noticing specific costumes. You may like the story the movie tells, the emotions it reveals, or the special effects it employs.

Just as you can appreciate the components of a movie and the finished product, you can enjoy a poem on several levels. Some poems are more difficult to understand than others, but the richer and deeper a poem, the more likely it is to yield several meanings.

All poetry, however, is not serious and profound. In this unit you will study poems that are humorous and entertaining. "Jabberwocky," for example, is a nonsense poem filled with made-up words and imaginary creatures. "The Milkmaid" is a humorous ballad, and "Blowin' in the Wind" is a popular song.

In this unit you will also read poems from contrasting cultures and backgrounds. No matter what language poets use, their poems contain ideas that people everywhere can understand.

Chapter 10

Selections

Jabberwocky
LEWIS CARROLL

The Milkmaid
TRADITIONAL

Blowin' in the Wind
BOB DYLAN

Lesson

Light Verse and Ballads

About the Selections

Many people think of poetry only as something to be studied in school or recited on certain formal occasions. Yet poetry can offer pleasure to anyone. In your childhood you heard poetry, although you may not have called it that. Nursery rhymes, such as Mother Goose rhymes, and lullabies, such as "Rock-a-bye Baby," are poetry. Even before most children go to school, they know "Hickory-Dickory-Dock," "Three Blind Mice," and "Humpty Dumpty." Those poems—many of them set to music—have entertained people for hundreds of years. They belong in a category of poetry called <u>light verse</u>—poetry that uses an ordinary speaking voice and a relaxed manner to treat its subject cheerfully, comically, or with ridicule.

Light verse is humorous in many ways. Sometimes it tells an amusing tale that offers a lesson. At other times it satirizes, or makes fun of, human foolishness. One type of light verse is the nonsense poem, in which sense is less important than the sounds of the words.

The first poem you will read, Lewis Carroll's "Jabberwocky," is one of the best-known nonsense poems. The title itself suggests that humor may be important in the poem. "Jabberwocky" appears in Lewis Carroll's famous book *Through the Looking-Glass,* the sequel to *Alice's Adventures in Wonderland.* Both works relate the fantastic adventures of a girl named Alice who suddenly finds herself in a strange land filled with bizarre characters.

In *Through the Looking-Glass* Alice steps through a mirror into a world where everything is reversed. She picks up a book from a table and glances through it, only to discover she cannot read its strange language. Then she suddenly realizes that it is "a looking-glass book." Holding a page to a mirror, she reads the poem "Jabberwocky."

The second poem, "The Milkmaid," is a well-known folk song from the American South. Like many American folk songs, however, its origins can be traced to England. "The Milkmaid" is a ballad—a song that tells a simple story. Many ballads have been passed from generation to generation by word of mouth before being written down. Popular ballads were sometimes carried long distances by travelers or, as in the case of "The Milkmaid," by settlers who voyaged from England to North America. Over time, the stories told in the ballads often underwent some changes, but the basic narratives remained the same. As you will read, "The Milkmaid" tells about a simple, humorous encounter between a pretty milkmaid and a stranger.

The last selection, Bob Dylan's "Blowin' in the Wind," also has elements of a traditional folk ballad. It is an example of a broadside ballad—a ballad composed to address a current event or issue. Although you are reading it as a poem, Dylan composed it as a song in 1962. You may be familiar with its melody, because "Blowin' in the Wind" was among the most popular songs of the 1960s and is still frequently played.

Lewis Carroll, the author of "Jabberwocky," is the pen name of Charles Lutwidge Dodgson. As Lewis Carroll, he has delighted several generations of children and adults with his two *Alice* books. As Charles Dodgson, however, he was a serious mathematician and the author of several books on mathematics. Dodgson, who was born in 1832 and died in 1898, spent most of his life teaching mathematics at Oxford University in England. It was there that the *Alice* books were created.

Dodgson was friendly with Alice Liddell, the young daughter of the dean of one of the colleges at Oxford. On a July day in 1862, Dodgson and a friend took Alice and her sisters rowing. Dodgson had often entertained the children by inventing stories. That day he began telling the story of a character named Alice and how she fell down a rabbit hole into a fantastic "wonderland." There she had many strange adventures and met characters like the Cheshire Cat, the Mad Hatter, and the Mock Turtle.

At Alice Liddell's insistence, Carroll wrote out the story and later expanded it into its present book length. The book is still very popular and has been translated into over thirty languages.

To young people of the 1960s, Bob Dylan was a symbol of the protest movements of that decade. Dylan, whose real name is Robert Zimmerman, was born in Duluth, Minnesota, in 1941. As a teenager, he learned to play the guitar, the piano, and the harmonica. In 1960 he visited New York City, and there he met the famous composer and folk singer Woody Guthrie. Under Guthrie's influence, Dylan developed his own musical tastes and style.

In 1963 Dylan met Joan Baez, a popular folk singer who toured the country with him and helped launch his career. Dylan composed many songs that focused on social problems and injustices. Among his best-known compositions are "Blowin' in the Wind," "The Times They Are A'Changin'," and "Like a Rolling Stone."

Lesson Preview

The lesson that follows the three poems focuses on the appeal of light verse and ballads. People enjoy reading and hearing poetry for a number of reasons. In some poems the humor or the story is appealing. In others the imagery, rhythm, and sounds are striking. Often the subject and the theme of a poem is particularly significant. The most popular poems usually combine several of these characteristics.

The questions that follow will help you to appreciate the nature of a poem's appeal. As you read, think about how you would answer these questions.

1 What happens in "Jabberwocky"? What elements of the poem are humorous? What effect do the invented words have on the poem?

2 What is the story of "The Milkmaid"? What is humorous about the poem?

3 What is the structure of "Blowin' in the Wind"? What distinguishes Dylan's song from the other two poems in this chapter?

Note: The poems in this chapter do not have difficult vocabulary.

Jabberwocky

LEWIS CARROLL

'Twas brillig, and the slithy toves
    Did gyre and gimble in the wabe:
All mimsy were the borogoves,
    And the mome raths outgrabe.

5   "Beware the Jabberwock, my son!
    The jaws that bite, the claws that catch!
Beware the Jubjub bird, and shun
    The frumious Bandersnatch!"

He took his vorpal sword in hand:
10   Long time the manxome foe he sought—
So rested he by the Tumtum tree,
    And stood awhile in thought.

And, as in uffish thought he stood,
    The Jabberwock, with eyes of flame,
15   Came whiffling through the tulgey wood,
    And burbled as it came!

One, two! One, two! And through and through
    The vorpal blade went snicker-snack!
He left it dead, and with its head
20   He went galumphing back.

"And, hast thou slain the Jabberwock?
    Come to my arms, my beamish boy!
O frabjous day! Callooh! Callay!"
    He chortled in his joy.

25 'Twas brillig, and the slithy toves
Did gyre and gimble in the wabe:
All mimsy were the borogoves,
And the mome raths outgrabe.

The Milkmaid

TRADITIONAL

"Where are you going, my pretty little fair maid,
Red rosy cheeks and curly black hair?"
"I'm going a-milking," so kind-like she answered him.
Sailing in the dew makes a milkmaid fair

5 "What is your father, my pretty little fair maid,
Red rosy cheeks and curly black hair?"
"My father's a farmer," so kind-like she answered him.
Sailing in the dew makes a milkmaid fair

"What is your mother, my pretty little fair maid,
10   Red rosy cheeks and curly black hair?"
"My mother's a weaver," so kind-like she answered him.
Sailing in the dew makes a milkmaid fair

"What is your fortune, my pretty little fair maid,
Red rosy cheeks and curly black hair?"
15 "My face is my fortune," so kind-like she answered him.
Sailing in the dew makes a milkmaid fair

"Then I will not marry you, my pretty little fair maid,
Red, rosy cheeks and curly black hair."
"Nobody cares, sir," so kind-like she answered him.
20   Sailing in the dew makes a milkmaid fair

Light Verse and Ballads

Blowin' in the Wind

Bob Dylan

How many roads must a man walk down
Before you call him a man?
Yes, 'n' how many seas must a white dove sail
Before she sleeps in the sand?
5 Yes, 'n' how many times must the cannon balls fly
Before they're forever banned?
The answer, my friend, is blowin' in the wind,
The answer is blowin' in the wind.

How many times must a man look up
10 Before he can see the sky?
Yes, 'n' how many ears must one man have
Before he can hear people cry?
Yes, 'n' how many deaths will it take till he knows
That too many people have died?
15 The answer, my friend, is blowin' in the wind,
The answer is blowin' in the wind.

How many years can a mountain exist
Before it's washed to the sea?
Yes, 'n' how many years can some people exist
20 Before they're allowed to be free?
Yes, 'n' how many times can a man turn his head,
Pretending he just doesn't see?
The answer, my friend, is blowin' in the wind,
The answer is blowin' in the wind.

Reviewing the Selections

Answer each of the following questions. You may look back at the poems if necessary.

Recalling Facts

1. In "Jabberwocky" the boy slays the Jabberwock by
   - ☐ a. trapping it in the tulgey wood.
   - ☐ b. running it through with his vorpal blade.
   - ☐ c. hitting it with the Tumtum tree.
   - ☐ d. choking it in his arms.

Understanding Main Ideas

2. The speaker's questions in "Blowin' in the Wind" are aimed at
   - ☐ a. exposing corruption.
   - ☐ b. showing that most of life's questions can be answered.
   - ☐ c. making people think about peace and freedom.
   - ☐ d. showing that death threatens everyone.

Placing Events in Order

3. In "The Milkmaid" the man asks about the maid's fortune
   - ☐ a. after she turns him down.
   - ☐ b. before he asks about her father.
   - ☐ c. before he asks where she is going.
   - ☐ d. after he asks about her parents.

Finding Supporting Details

4. What are the Jabberwock's main features?
   - ☐ a. jaws, claws, and flaming eyes
   - ☐ b. long tail and huge wings
   - ☐ c. arms like the tentacles of an octopus
   - ☐ d. the ability to breathe fire and burble loudly

5. "Yes, 'n' how many times must the cannon balls
   fly / Before they're forever <u>banned</u>?" In this
   context *banned* means
   ☐ a. organized.
   ☐ b. approved.
   ☐ c. forgotten.
   ☐ d. forbidden.

Interpreting the Selections

Answer each of the following questions. You may look back at the poems if necessary.

*Making
Inferences*

6. "The answer is blowin' in the wind." That line
   probably means that the answers to important
   questions are
   ☐ a. carefully documented.
   ☐ b. insignificant, but interesting.
   ☐ c. unimportant.
   ☐ d. available for you to find.

*Analyzing
the Evidence*

7. In "Jabberwocky" the boy's father is
   ☐ a. delighted by his son's venture.
   ☐ b. angry with him for killing the Jabberwock.
   ☐ c. a distant, reserved figure.
   ☐ d. a mocking, unkind person.

8. In "Blowin' in the Wind" the speaker wants his audience to be more
   - ☐ a. decisive.
   - ☐ b. reasonable.
   - ☐ c. caring about humanity.
   - ☐ d. understanding toward their children.

9. "The Milkmaid" and "Blowin' in the Wind" are alike in that both
   - ☐ a. have a light, humorous tone.
   - ☐ b. concern love and marriage.
   - ☐ c. are made up of questions and answers.
   - ☐ d. have two speakers.

10. In "The Milkmaid" the man wants the girl's
    - ☐ a. love.
    - ☐ b. fortune.
    - ☐ c. farm.
    - ☐ d. cows.

Light Verse
and Ballads

If you think about your favorite poems, you may recall certain lines or images. You may even have memorized some lines or stanzas. Memorization makes a poem part of your own imagination, and it creates a unique bond between you and the poet.

Each of the poems in this chapter has gained a special place in the imaginations of many people. Why are the poems memorable? Why do they still appeal to readers and listeners long after they were written? In this lesson you will learn why certain poems have maintained their popular appeal.

"Jabberwocky": Reading for Meaning

Your first reaction after reading Lewis Carroll's poem may have been one of confusion. Does the poem make any kind of sense? The poem has a straight-forward narrative, or story, hidden behind the nonsense words: Somewhere there is a fantastic place. Among its inhabitants are slithy toves, Jubjub birds, and a frumious Bandersnatch. The most fearsome creature of all is the Jabberwock, with its "jaws that bite," "claws that catch," and "eyes of flame." A brave boy, armed with "his vorpal sword," goes in search of the monster. After a long hunt, he finally meets the Jabberwock by the Tumtum tree. He slays the beast, cuts off its head, and returns home in triumph.

The events of the narrative recall the stories of legendary dragon-killing heroes. Like the heroes in those old stories, the boy goes forth lightly armed to meet his fate, despite the warnings of his elder. Even though the poem describes a dangerous encounter, everything about it is touched with humor; you never fear for the boy's life. The poem is a <u>parody</u>, a type of humorous writing in which a writer ridicules a serious literary subject. In "Jabberwocky" Carroll parodies narrative poems that tell of ancient heroes.

1. What is humorous about the setting and the story of "Jabberwocky"?

Even though the Jabberwock is supposed to be a dangerous monster, it does not seem at all dangerous when it appears. The boy does not seem particularly heroic, either.

2. What details does Lewis Carroll mention that make each character something less than fearful or heroic?

Sound Appeal

Much of the pleasure in reading or hearing "Jabberwocky" comes from the sound of the poem. Like most nonsense verse, "Jabberwocky" has a strong rhythm and a simple rhyme scheme. Those elements give it a songlike quality that makes the poem easy to remember.

Read the first stanza, which is repeated as a refrain at the end of the poem. Even though most of the words seem to make no sense, they introduce many strange and interesting sounds.

3. Read stanza 1 several times. What examples do you find of alliteration, assonance, and rhyme? How do the sounds of that stanza create a mood, or a general atmosphere, in the poem?

4. Scan stanza 5 and describe the meter. What effect does the meter have on the way you read the poem?

5. What is the rhyme scheme of "Jabberwocky"?

Humorous Language and Images

Most of the appeal of "Jabberwocky" is contained in the made-up words. Several of these words are what Lewis Carroll called "portmanteau words."

Portmanteau is a French word meaning a traveling bag with two compartments. A portmanteau word is a word that packs, or combines, the meanings of two words into one. *Smog,* for example, is a portmanteau word made up of *smoke* and *fog.* Carroll once explained how the word *frumious* (line 8) was invented:

> . . . take the two words "fuming" and "furious." Make up your mind that you will say both words, but leave it unsettled which you will say first. Now open your mouth and speak. If your thoughts incline ever so little towards "fuming," you will say "fuming-furious"; if they turn, by even a hair's breadth, towards "furious," you will say "furious-fuming"; but if you have the rarest of gifts, a perfectly balanced mind, you will say "frumious."

In *Through the Looking-Glass* Alice meets Humpty Dumpty and asks him to explain the meaning of "Jabberwocky." In an extended analysis he explains that *slithy* means "lithe and slimy" and that *mimsy* is "flimsy and miserable." Other made-up words in Carroll's poems are not portmanteau words, but refer to a single thing. *Toves,* for example, "are something like badgers," according to Humpty Dumpty. But you probably have your own ideas about what the invented words mean.

You can tell that the Bandersnatch and the Jabberwock are fictional creatures, and Carroll gives you just enough detail to let you create your own image of them.

6. Describe the picture you have of the Bandersnatch and of the Jabberwock. Which is the more frightening? Why?

The Folk Ballad

The second poem, "The Milkmaid," is a folk ballad. As you have read, a ballad is a song that tells a simple story. A ballad usually concentrates on a single dramatic incident or situation. It has few characters, and the story is often developed through dialogue, or the actual conversation between the characters.

Ballads commonly contain several elements. One of these elements is a refrain—one or more lines that are repeated regularly throughout a poem. A refrain makes a poem easier to remember because of the predictability of repeated words or phrases.

Another element common to ballads is an epithet. An <u>epithet</u> is a descriptive word or phrase that expresses a quality or a characteristic of an object or person. The Russian czar Ivan IV was called "Ivan the Terrible." "The Terrible" is an epithet. In a ballad an epithet is a name tag that appears each time a particular character speaks. Like a refrain, the epithet is predictable and makes characters easy to remember.

Finally, ballads have familiar subjects. Many ballads tell of faithful or unfaithful lovers or of courageous actions by heroic men and women. Some ballads end with a tragic or comic twist.

"The Milkmaid" fits the pattern of a traditional folk ballad. The situation is simple and dramatic: A stranger accosts a pretty young farm girl on her way to milk the cows. Through dialogue, you learn something about her, although almost nothing about him. From his questions, you begin to suspect that his motives in talking to the girl are questionable. When he asks, "What is your fortune, my pretty little fair maid," you sense his dishonorable character and intentions. He will not marry her, he says in the last stanza, for she has no fortune.

Then comes the humorous twist. Instead of the expected ending—an innocent girl left helplessly in love with a stranger—you meet a girl who is very capable of taking care of herself.

7. What is the milkmaid's response to the man's refusal to marry her? How have you been prepared for the girl's frank response?

The Ballad's Appeal

The appeal of "The Milkmaid" is different from that of "Jabberwocky." Lewis Carroll's poem offers a mixture of fantasy, adventure, and humorous language. Although there is certainly humor in the last stanza of "The Milkmaid," the poem's attraction lies primarily in its simple, direct story. "The Milkmaid" is easy to understand, and the story is appealingly presented as a gradual revelation, through a series of questions and answers. The story also has an element of <u>suspense</u>—the interest, excitement, and anticipation you feel about what will happen in the story.

The ballad ends humorously, at the expense of the stranger. Like so much folk humor, it demonstrates that country people are much wiser than many people think.

8. Examine the refrains and the epithets in "The Milkmaid." In what ways do you think they add to the ballad's appeal?

A Contemporary Ballad

Bob Dylan's folk song "Blowin' in the Wind" also contains some elements of the traditional ballad.

9. Compare Dylan's folk song and "The Milkmaid." What elements are similar?

Despite the similarities, "Blowin' in the Wind" differs in many ways from traditional ballads. It has no characters beyond the speaker. The poem does not have a narrative, but instead focuses on several questions about life, nature, and society.

The speaker assures you that the answers to his questions are "blowin' in the wind." The answers are out there, all around you, available to you if you care enough to find them. The theme, or underlying message, of the song is that you *must* find the answers, just as you *must not* ignore the questions.

10. How does Dylan involve you in the issues and answers?

Origins of "Blowin' in the Wind"

Bob Dylan's song is firmly rooted in real events. As you have read, Dylan was actively engaged in the protest movements of the 1960s that focused international attention on social injustices. The protests addressed problems such as discrimination against minorities and the war in Vietnam.

Dylan and his contemporaries believed that the world must be changed. They were convinced that their protests against war, inequality, and injustice would make a difference. That idealism is reflected in the music of the times.

11. Why does "Blowin' in the Wind" still retain its appeal?

Ideas and Images

Bob Dylan's song poses a number of profound questions that are not easily answered.

12. Read the first two questions that Dylan poses. What does each question mean? Why are the questions difficult to answer?

13. Why is the third question in stanza 1 both simple and difficult to answer?

The language of the poem is deceptively simple. Yet through the questions followed by a single answer, Dylan creates a series of powerful images. The images, like the questions, suggest different levels of meaning.

The last stanza begins: "How many years can a mountain exist / Before it's washed to the sea?" On the surface level, you see the enormous rocky bulk of a mountain steadily worn down by erosion until it gradually reaches sea level. On a deeper level, the image suggests something whose size and strength should make it able to withstand any beating. Despite its apparent strength, it cannot withstand the constant battering of forces that wears it down to nothing.

That question is raised again in the next two lines, but this time it is related to people. The images in those four lines suggest that the speaker is talking about discrimination, slavery, bigotry, and inequality.

14. Think about one of the questions. What image does it contain? Can that image be interpreted on more than one level? Explain your answer.

Questions for Thought and Discussion

The questions and activities that follow will help you explore the three poems in this chapter in more depth and at the same time develop your critical thinking skills.

1. **Analyzing Language.** Divide the class into six small groups. Each group should take one stanza of "Jabberwocky" and make a list of all the nonsense words in that stanza. Decide which words on your list are portmanteau words and try to decide what words they are made up of. Then decide what the other nonsense words in the stanza might mean. Share your group's ideas with the rest of the class.

2. **Analyzing Character.** What do you learn about the character of the young farm girl in "The Milkmaid"? Find evidence in the poem to support your answer.

3. **Comparing.** Compare the tone—the poet's attitude toward his or her subject and audience—in "Jabberwocky" and "Blowin' in the Wind." Then explain how the tone contributes to the mood, or general atmosphere, of the poem.

Writing About Literature

Several suggestions for writing projects are given below. You may be asked to complete one or more of these projects. If you have any questions about how to begin a writing assignment, review Using the Writing Process, beginning on page 219.

1. **Writing a Description.** Picture what you think the Jabberwock looks like. Then, in a paragraph or two, describe the Jabberwock so that others can visualize how you imagine it. Your description can be either humorous (you might use portmanteau words) or serious.

2. **Reviewing a Poem.** Imagine that you are a reviewer who has read one of the poems in this chapter for the first time. Write a brief review of the poem, analyzing its strengths and its weaknesses and explaining why you think it will remain popular for a long time.

3. **Creating a Ballad.** Choose a recent event to be the subject of a ballad. In a paragraph explain the story that your ballad will tell. Then write one or more verses of the ballad. Use some common elements of a ballad, such as dialogue, a refrain, and epithets.

4. **Comparing.** Think of a popular song of today. Then compare that song to "Blowin' in the Wind." To whom is each song addressed? How are the songs similar? How are they different? Which do you think will still be popular in fifty years? Why?

Chapter 11

Selections

Song for the Sun That Disappeared Behind the Rainclouds

TRADITIONAL KHOIKHOI SONG

Clear Evening After Rain

TU FU

The Moon Rises

FEDERICO GARCÍA LORCA

Lesson

Comparing Three Lyric Poems

About the Selections

People from every country and culture have made poetry. Even before writing was developed, people created forms of poetry in songs and chants. After writing was invented, poems began to be recorded, and poets became more concerned with the structure of their works. Yet the basic elements of poetry remained the same, and people continued to express their feelings, ideas, and thoughts through their poems.

The poems in this chapter come from three very different cultures. The first poem, "Song for the Sun That Disappeared Behind the Rainclouds," is a traditional song of the Khoikhoi, a group of people living in southwestern Africa. The second poem, "Clear Evening After Rain," was written by an eighth-century Chinese poet. The third selection, "The Moon Rises," is the work of a twentieth-century poet. Despite their different origins, the three poems are all concerned with nature.

Many poets have celebrated nature. In "Fern Hill," "Pied Beauty," and "Birches," for example, you learned how Dylan Thomas, Gerard Manley Hopkins, and Robert Frost considered patterns of life and nature. Each of the three poems in this chapter responds to an event in nature, and each expresses its own attitude toward nature and the relationship between people and the natural world.

The first poem reflects the traditions of the nomadic Khoikhoi, whose daily lives were closely influenced by nature. The Khoikhoi were one of several groups who migrated into southern Africa hundreds of years ago. *Khoikhoi,* which means "men of men," is the people's own name for themselves. Early European settlers called them Hottentots, perhaps in imitation of the distinctive clicking sounds in the Khoikhoi language. Anthropologists believe that about eighteen Khoikhoi tribes once flourished in southern Africa. But warfare, disease, and intermarriage gradually destroyed the Khoikhoi, and today only one Khoikhoi group, the Nama, remains. They live in Namibia in southwest Africa. From that group comes the poem you will read.

Tu Fu, who lived from 712 to 770, is considered by many people to be one of China's greatest poets. He was born into a family of scholars and government officials during the T'ang dynasty. Under the T'ang, China enjoyed prosperity and great achievements in the arts.

Tu Fu received a traditional education, studying the works of ancient scholars, especially those of Confucius. That education was meant to prepare him for the competitive examinations that would allow him to enter the imperial civil service. Tu Fu, however, was unable to pass the civil service tests and consequently could not be granted an official position. He spent much of his youth traveling, composing poetry as he wandered. When he returned home, he again failed to pass the imperial examinations.

About the year 752, Tu Fu married and settled on a farm. He held several minor government jobs, but like many Chinese, he experienced periods of severe hardship. During one lean period, several of his children died of starvation. Toward the end of his life, Tu Fu returned to wandering, living on a river in a houseboat in which he slowly floated south. Although he wrote poems about many subjects, Tu Fu is best remembered for his early works, which celebrated the beauty of the natural world and lamented the passing of time.

Federico García Lorca was both a poet and a dramatist. He is among the most celebrated Spanish writers of the twentieth century. García Lorca was born in 1898 into a wealthy farming family near Granada, Spain. As a child he demonstrated a gift for music, so his mother taught him to play the piano.

In school he showed a strong interest in literature, painting, and music. He composed and performed music, and even exhibited his paintings in Barcelona. About 1919, however, he realized that his real talent was literature.

At the University of Madrid, García Lorca became friends with other writers and artists, including the painter Salvador Dali and the filmmaker Luis Buñuel. He began to give poetry readings that made him famous throughout Spain. García Lorca published very little of his work. "Verse is made to be recited," he argued. "In a book it is dead."

García Lorca was intrigued by the folk and gypsy ballads of his native Andalusia, the region of Spain in which his family had lived for generations. From those ballads, he drew the inspiration for much of his poetry and drama. Yet he was also influenced by the modern trends of surrealism, a literary and artistic movement of the 1920s and 1930s. Surrealists tried to free themselves from the control of reason and convention. Instead, they drew their ideas and forms from dreams and the free association of words. As a result, the works of surrealists often seem wild, mysterious, and dreamlike.

Spain in the 1930s was politically divided between right-wing Fascists and leftists. Although García Lorca was not politically active, he associated with many liberals and leftists. When the Fascists gained power, his books were banned, then burned in public. In 1936 after the outbreak of the Spanish Civil War, García Lorca went into hiding, but was soon captured by Fascist soldiers. One night he was taken out, forced to dig his own grave, and then shot.

Lesson Preview

The lesson that follows compares and contrasts the three lyric poems. A lyric poem, you will recall, is a poem that expresses a deeply felt thought or emotion. Each of the poems you will read has been translated into English from another language. However, the translators have tried to preserve the images and the moods of the original poems.

The questions that follow will help you to identify the view of nature that each poem presents. As you read, think about how you would answer these questions.

1 What event inspired each poem?

2 In "Song for the Sun That Disappeared Behind the Rainclouds," how are natural events related to ordinary human activities?

3 In "Clear Evening After Rain" what natural occurrences are described? What human activities are described?

4 In "The Moon Rises" what are the main images? What feelings do those images suggest?

Note: The poems in this chapter do not contain difficult vocabulary.

Song for the Sun That Disappeared Behind the Rainclouds

TRADITIONAL KHOIKHOI POEM

The fire darkens, the wood turns black.
The flame extinguishes, misfortune upon us.
God sets out in search of the sun.
The rainbow sparkles in his hand,
5 the bow of the divine hunter.
He has heard the lamentations of his children.
He walks along the milky way, he collects the stars.
With quick arms he piles them into a basket
piles them up with quick arms
10 like a woman who collects lizards
and piles them into her pot, piles them
until the pot overflows with lizards
until the basket overflows with light.

Clear Evening After Rain

TU FU

Translated by Kenneth Rexroth

The sun sinks towards the horizon.
The light clouds are blown away.
A rainbow shines on the river.
The last raindrops spatter the rocks.
5 Cranes and herons soar in the sky.
Fat bears feed along the banks.

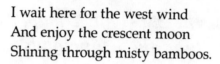

I wait here for the west wind
And enjoy the crescent moon
Shining through misty bamboos.

The Moon Rises

Federico García Lorca

Translated by William B. Logan

When the moon comes up
the bells are lost
and there appear
impenetrable paths.

5   When the moon comes up
the sea blankets the earth
and the heart feels
like an island in infinity.

No one eats oranges
10 under the full moon.
One must eat
cold green fruit.

When the moon comes up
with a hundred equal faces,
15 silver money
sobs in the pocket.

Reviewing the Selections

Answer each of the following questions. You may look back at the poems if necessary.

Recalling Facts
1. In "Song for the Sun That Disappeared Behind the Rainclouds," who restores light to the world?
   - ☐ a. a woman
   - ☐ b. God
   - ☐ c. the lizards
   - ☐ d. the children

Understanding Main Ideas
2. In "Clear Evening After Rain" the speaker is
   - ☐ a. dreaming.
   - ☐ b. intent on writing poetry.
   - ☐ c. enjoying a peaceful moment in nature.
   - ☐ d. observing the effects of rain on the crops.

Placing Events in Order
3. In "Song for the Sun That Disappeared Behind the Rainclouds," what happened after the sun disappeared?
   - ☐ a. It rained.
   - ☐ b. The moon rose.
   - ☐ c. All became dark.
   - ☐ d. A rainbow appeared.

Finding Supporting Details
4. According to García Lorca's poem, when the moon is full, one must
   - ☐ a. pick fresh oranges.
   - ☐ b. sit by the ocean.
   - ☐ c. walk down dark paths.
   - ☐ d. eat cold green fruit.

Comparing Three Lyric Poems

5. "When the moon comes up / the bells are lost / and there appear / <u>impenetrable</u> paths." In this context *impenetrable* means
   - ☐ a. impassable.
   - ☐ b. undiscoverable.
   - ☐ c. twisting.
   - ☐ d. frightening.

Interpreting the Selections

Answer each of the following questions. You may look back at the poems if necessary.

6. In "Song for the Sun That Disappeared Behind the Rainclouds," the people regard God as
   - ☐ a. an angry force to be appeased.
   - ☐ b. a raincloud.
   - ☐ c. a helper and a defender.
   - ☐ d. a friendly but passive force.

7. The images in "Clear Evening After Rain" indicate that the speaker feels
   - ☐ a. nervous.
   - ☐ b. peaceful.
   - ☐ c. confused.
   - ☐ d. overjoyed.

8. In "The Moon Rises" García Lorca seems
   to want to
   - ☐ a. capture the emotional effect of
     the moonrise.
   - ☐ b. describe the physical changes in the
     landscape during the moonrise.
   - ☐ c. re-create the sounds and aromas of the
     Spanish night.
   - ☐ d. show how different day and night are.

Comparing

9. In both "Clear Evening After Rain" and
   "The Moon Rises," a moon rises. However, the
   moods of the poems are different. Which pair of
   adjectives best summarizes the different moods
   of the two poems?
   - ☐ a. humorous—serious
   - ☐ b. playful—critical
   - ☐ c. bitter—accepting
   - ☐ d. tranquil—intense

Drawing
Conclusions

10. In "The Moon Rises" the speaker views nature as
    - ☐ a. quiet and elegant.
    - ☐ b. eccentric but not dangerous.
    - ☐ c. overpowering and unpredictable.
    - ☐ d. mysterious and somewhat frightening.

Comparing Three Lyric Poems

Lyric poems, as you have learned, express a deeply felt thought or emotion. Each of the three lyric poems you have just read concerns an event in nature. The event, however, is less important than the speaker's feelings about it. In this lesson you will compare the feelings developed in the poem and the ways in which those feelings are expressed. Comparing and contrasting poems helps you to distinguish the unique qualities of a poem and at the same time judge the poem in relation to other poems.

"Song for the Sun That Disappeared Behind the Rainclouds": Reading for Meaning

The title of this traditional Khoikhoi song introduces a dramatic event: The sun disappears. The poem tells the story of what happens when the sun disappears behind rainclouds. The sky darkens and the rains come. Hearing the sorrowful cries of his children over the loss of light, God goes in search of the sun. He collects stars in a basket, and when the basket is full, light overflows and the sun again illuminates the earth.

1. What can you infer about the relationship between the people and nature?

Imagery, Mood, and Theme

The poem is far more than a simple narrative. It is filled with vivid imagery that supports the people's strong faith in God. To understand the feelings conveyed by the poem, you need to examine those images. The images in the first two lines, for example, help you to clearly visualize the sun's disappearance and the rainfall:

> The fire darkens, the wood turns black.
> The flame extinguishes, misfortune upon us.

Those lines have two levels of meaning. On the surface level, the fire is a campfire, the central hearth around which the people gather. The darkening of the fire and the extinguishing of its flame results from the rainfall. The loss of the fire is a severe misfortune to the nomadic hunting and herding people. On a deeper level, the darkened fire and the extinguished flame are metaphors for the sun.

Most of the poem is devoted to images of God. He is given human characteristics even though He is divine.

2. What images suggest that God has human characteristics? What feelings about God do those images convey?

God is a powerful force, yet He is not frightening. His actions are human, despite His power.

3. Think about the simile developed in lines 8 through 13. What is the feeling created by that simile?

The imagery of the Khoikhoi song creates the mood of the poem and suggests its theme. During the course of the poem, the mood changes. In the opening lines there is a sense of disaster and urgency. The disappearance of the sun is a calamity. With the appearance of God, however, the mood lightens. "God sets out in search of the sun." He is carrying a rainbow, a joyful symbol of returning light, full of color and hope. By the end of the poem, the basket—and the world—are overflowing with light.

4. Reread the poem and then explain its theme. Remember that the images in a poem support the theme.

The Mood of "Clear Evening After Rain"

On the surface, Tu Fu's poem contains some of the same images as the Khoikhoi song: the disappearing sun, a sudden rainfall, and a shining rainbow. Yet the poems are very different in mood and theme.

The first six lines of "Clear Evening After Rain" simply record the speaker's observations about the evening. Each line contains one impression: the setting sun, clouds blown by the breeze, a rainbow reflected on the river, raindrops falling upon the rocks, water birds rising into the sky, bears feeding along the riverbanks. In the last three lines the speaker shifts from recording his observations to analyzing his feelings.

5. Describe the mood in the first six lines. What are the speaker's feelings in the last three lines?

Imagery and Theme

The imagery in Tu Fu's poem is less dramatic than the imagery in "Song for the Sun." In the Khoikhoi song you feel that nature can be threatening. If the sun disappears suddenly, there is "misfortune." The people are not at ease with nature; they worry about its effects. In Tu Fu's poem, by contrast, you feel that nature is gentle and restful. The solitary speaker in the poem is relaxed, waiting for a breeze and enjoying the sight of the moon. The imagery is simple and direct, and it does not rely on figurative language.

6. Review the imagery and mood of Tu Fu's poem. Then explain the poem's theme. How does the theme compare to that of "Song for the Sun"?

"The Moon Rises": Reading for Meaning

Like the first two poems, Federico García Lorca's poem concerns nature. Yet in "The Moon Rises," a sense of strangeness and mystery envelops the poem. The scene is the world as it appears in moonlight. When the moon rises— especially a full moon—things look and seem very different from the way they appear in daylight.

Read stanza 1. When the moon rises, "the bells are lost / and there appear / impenetrable paths." By day you can see the bells, but at night the bells are hidden in shadow. Like the bells, paths that in daylight are easy to see become hard to follow at night. In the moonlight you may see the entrance to a path, but you cannot see where it leads.

7. What mood is established in the first stanza of "The Moon Rises"?

Stanza 2 develops a new image of the world seen by moonlight. As you may know, the moon and the tides are closely connected. In this stanza the speaker refers to the incoming tides: "When the moon comes up / the sea blankets the earth."

8. What metaphor is the speaker using in line 6?

9. What feeling does the simile in lines 7 and 8 create?

Stanza 3 presents a startling concrete image. "Under the full moon," the speaker says, "No one eats oranges." Instead, "One must eat / cold green fruit." Oranges are associated with sunlight and warmth. Cold green fruit, by contrast, suggests the mysterious mood of the full moon.

In the last stanza the poet creates two strange and apparently unconnected images. One image is a series of images created by the reflections of the moonlight, "with a hundred equal faces." The other is the sound of "silver money" that "sobs in the pocket." Silver is a color associated both with moonlight and with money.

10. Reread the last stanza several times, carefully studying the imagery. What does the stanza mean?

Imagery, Mood, and Theme

Both "Song for the Sun That Disappeared Behind the Rainclouds" and "Clear Evening After Rain" are more straightforward than "The Moon Rises." García Lorca approaches nature in a way that is not strictly logical or even realistic. The images in the poem reflect its dreamlike, mysterious mood—lost bells, impenetrable paths, cold green fruit, and money that "sobs in the pocket."

In "The Moon Rises" nature is neither threatening nor pleasant: It is a reflection of imagination, moods, and emotions. The speaker observes a world that mirrors his feelings. He translates his feelings into images. The images are beautiful, dreamlike, and illogical, but they nonetheless reveal the speaker's inner self.

11. What is the theme of the poem? What attitude toward nature does the poem reveal?

Questions for Thought and Discussion

The questions and activities that follow will help you explore the three poems in this chapter in more depth and at the same time develop your critical thinking skills.

1. **Identifying the Speaker and the Audience.** Who is the speaker in "Song for the Sun That Disappeared Behind the Rainclouds"? Who is the intended audience? What is the speaker's attitude toward God?

2. **Analyzing Character.** What do you learn about the character of the speaker in Tu Fu's poem "Clear Evening After Rain"? Be as specific as possible, supporting your analysis with words, phrases, and images from the poem.

3. **Interpreting Mood.** What is the mood of "The Moon Rises"? Does the mood change from stanza to stanza? Explain your answer.

4. **Expressing an Opinion.** Think about the view of nature expressed in each of the three poems in this chapter. With which view of nature do you feel most comfortable? Explain your opinion.

5. **Comparing.** Compare Tu Fu's poem "Clear Evening After Rain" to the three haiku you read in Chapter 4. How is Tu Fu's poem similar to the three haiku? How is it different?

Writing About Literature

Several suggestions for writing projects follow. You may be asked to complete one or more of these projects. If you have any questions about how to begin a writing assignment, review Using the Writing Process, beginning on page 219.

1. **Describing an Event in Nature.** Choose a natural occurrence such as a sunrise, a thunderstorm, or a snowfall. Think about the mood it inspires in you and the images it suggests. Then write several paragraphs or a short poem in which you describe the event and at the same time communicate your feelings about it.

2. **Writing an Explanation.** Reflect for a few minutes about paintings, poems, and musical works that treat subjects in nature. Think about the themes in those works. In a page or two, explain why artists, poets, and musicians often choose natural subjects. Before you begin writing, make a list of your ideas and organize them in a logical way. Wherever possible, support your ideas with examples.

3. **Expressing an Opinion.** Choose an image that you like in one of the poems in this chapter. Explain why you like that image.

Chapter 12

Selections

From a Childhood
RAINER MARIA RILKE

Poem: Hate is only one
of many responses
FRANK O'HARA

Lesson

Communicating Through Poetry

About the Selections

Why do you read poetry? What do you hope to find in a poet's words? Perhaps you read poems for pleasure, as a form of entertainment or relaxation. Many people read poetry to learn from it. Poetry can help you to view and understand life in new ways.

Good poems are expressions of ideas and feelings that the poet wants to share with other people. Because poets are artists, they may be more perceptive about certain aspects of life than many people. Through their poetry, poets share their insights about the world. When you read a poem and share a poet's insights, you experience a sense of satisfaction as well as pleasure.

Reading a good poem is like traveling to a new place or spending time with a wise friend who has seen more of life than you have. When you travel, you see new sights and learn about other cultures through your own experiences. Listening to a friend, you learn about people and gain understanding through the insights of another. The new understandings you gain through poetry are not always complex. Many poems, such as Tu Fu's "Clear Evening After Rain," which you read in Chapter 11, are simple and contain only a single idea, image, or perception. In that poem Tu Fu re-creates the visual and emotional experience of an early evening after a rainstorm. If you savor that moment as you read the poem, then you have shared the experience with him.

The two poems that you will read in this chapter take different approaches to the basic human feelings of love and hate. In "From a Childhood" Rainer Maria Rilke creates an intense scene for you to observe. Even though you are only an observer, you cannot help but feel the deep attachment between mother and child. In Frank O'Hara's "Hate is only one of many responses," the speaker seems to address you directly, urging you to express your feelings freely.

Rainer Maria Rilke considered poetry his mission, and he lived his life fulfilling that mission. Rilke was born in 1875, in Prague, which today is the capital of Czechoslovakia. His childhood was unhappy, and he later called it a "primer of horror." Part of that horror was the five years he spent at a military academy, a school that stifled rather than encouraged the boy's artistic temperament.

In the 1890s young Rilke attended universities in Prague, Munich, and Berlin, and during those years he published his first volume of poems. His travels to Italy, Russia, France, and Spain brought him into contact with other writers and artists who greatly influenced him. In 1901 Rilke married a young artist who had been a student of the famous French sculptor Auguste Rodin. But Rilke needed solitude, which he believed was necessary for his art. Eighteen months later, the couple separated, although they remained on friendly terms, as their many letters show.

In the early 1900s Rilke spent two years in Paris as Rodin's secretary. Under Rodin's influence, Rilke became even more convinced of the need for dedication and discipline to perfect his art.

In addition to his volumes of poems, which he claimed were "dictated" to him during periods of intense creativity, Rilke wrote short stories, an autobiographical novel, and a biography of Rodin. In his later years he suffered from leukemia and withdrew into solitude. From 1919 until his death in 1926, he lived in Switzerland in the tower of a medieval castle. While picking flowers one day, he was pricked by a thorn and developed a fatal case of blood poisoning.

The second poem you will read is by Frank O'Hara. He titled it, as he did many of his other poems, simply with the word "Poem." To distinguish this poem from his others, it is often referred to by its first line.

Frank O'Hara's poetry is joyous, conversational, humorous, and very personal. Sometimes it seems to be about unimportant everyday things. One early poem begins, "Oh! Kangaroos, sequins, chocolate sodas! / You really are beautiful!" Within all O'Hara's poems is the assumption that whatever is happening at any given moment in the poet's thoughts and feelings is what is most valuable. That is why many of O'Hara's poems, including the one you will read in this chapter, seem spontaneous.

Frank O'Hara was born in Baltimore in 1926 but spent most of his life in New York City. He was involved in literature, poetry, and the visual arts. During the 1960s, he served as an assistant curator at the Museum of Modern Art in New York City. O'Hara died in 1966 at the age of forty, during his most creative period as a poet. Despite his premature death, O'Hara left behind a substantial number of poems that have influenced the generation of poets that succeeded him.

Lesson Preview

The lesson that follows the two poems focuses on the ways in which poets communicate their thoughts, feelings, and ideas through poetry. Like other writers, poets want to involve you in their ideas and thoughts. After reading a good poem, you may feel that you have gained an insight into some aspect of life.

The questions that follow will help you identify the feelings, thoughts, and ideas that the poems are communicating. As you read, think about how you would answer these questions.

1 In "From a Childhood" what mood does the poet create in the opening lines? How is that mood maintained throughout the poem? What response does that mood evoke from you?

2 What feelings do the boy and his mother share in "From a Childhood"? Why is the piano important in the poem?

3 What are the main points that Frank O'Hara is making in "Hate is only one of many responses"?

4 How does Frank O'Hara's speaker make feelings such as hate, unkindness, and meanness seem real?

Note: The poems in this chapter do not have difficult vocabulary.

From a Childhood

RAINER MARIA RILKE

Translated by M. D. Herter Norton

The darkening was like riches in the room
in which the boy, withdrawn and secret, sat.
And when his mother entered as in a dream,
a glass quivered in the silent cabinet.
5 She felt how the room had given her away,
and kissed her boy: Are you here? . . .
Then both gazed timidly towards the piano,
for many an evening she would play a song
in which the child was strangely deeply caught.

10 He sat quite still. His big gaze hung
upon her hand which, all bowed down by the ring,
as it were heavily in snowdrifts going,
over the white keys went.

Poem: Hate is only one of many responses

FRANK O'HARA

Hate is only one of many responses
true, hurt and hate go hand in hand
but why be afraid of hate, it is only there

think of filth, is it really awesome
5   neither is hate
don't be shy of unkindness, either
it's cleansing and allows you to be direct
like an arrow that feels something

out and out meanness, too, lets love breathe
10   you don't have to fight off getting in too deep
you can always get out if you're not too scared

an ounce of prevention's
enough to poison the heart
don't think of others
15   until you have thought of yourself, are true
all of these things, if you feel them
will be graced by a certain reluctance
and turn into gold

if felt by me, will be smilingly deflected
20   by your mysterious concern

Reviewing the Selections

Answer each of the following questions. You may look back at the poems if necessary.

Recalling Facts

1. In "From a Childhood" what gives the mother away when she enters the room?
   - ☐ a. the sound of her footsteps
   - ☐ b. a glass quivering in a cabinet
   - ☐ c. the boy's intuition
   - ☐ d. the sound of her voice

Understanding Main Ideas

2. In "Hate is only one of many responses," the speaker implies that we should
   - ☐ a. be honest and open about our feelings.
   - ☐ b. mix hatred and kindness.
   - ☐ c. avoid filth.
   - ☐ d. be cruel whenever we want to be.

Placing Events in Order

3. In "From a Childhood" the mother plays the piano
   - ☐ a. every morning.
   - ☐ b. only on weekends.
   - ☐ c. often in the evening.
   - ☐ d. whenever she and her son are alone.

Finding Supporting Details

4. In Frank O'Hara's poem the speaker says that our "reluctance" to be selfish will turn our selfish impulses into
   - ☐ a. filth.
   - ☐ b. an arrow with feelings.
   - ☐ c. meanness.
   - ☐ d. gold.

5. "And when his mother entered as in a dream, / a glass quivered in the silent cabinet." In this context *quivered* means
   - ☐ a. fell over.
   - ☐ b. smashed.
   - ☐ c. sang.
   - ☐ d. trembled.

Interpreting the Selections

Answer each of the following questions. You may look back at the poems if necessary.

6. In stanza 1 of "Hate is only one of many responses," the speaker might be thinking about
   - ☐ a. a relationship between two people ending.
   - ☐ b. a person's feelings about himself or herself.
   - ☐ c. two nations at war.
   - ☐ d. a person receiving a physical injury.

7. The atmosphere in the room in "From a Childhood" can best be described as
   - ☐ a. bubbling and happy.
   - ☐ b. hushed and fearful.
   - ☐ c. silent and miserable.
   - ☐ d. intimate and emotional.

8. Frank O'Hara compares hate to filth to show that
   - ☐ a. both are bad.
   - ☐ b. neither is as bad as it seems.
   - ☐ c. hatred is an unnatural occurrence.
   - ☐ d. hate is worse than filth.

Comparing

9. In "From a Childhood" when the boy sits alone, he is "withdrawn and secret." Then in the company of his mother, he feels
   - ☐ a. deep pleasure.
   - ☐ b. greater alienation than before.
   - ☐ c. barely contained excitement.
   - ☐ d. an unnatural shyness.

*Drawing
Conclusions*

10. At the end of Frank O'Hara's poem, the speaker thinks about his own negative feelings toward another person. He concludes that those feelings will be
    - ☐ a. understood by someone who truly cares about him.
    - ☐ b. understood but never forgiven.
    - ☐ c. used against him by other people.
    - ☐ d. ignored if he doesn't express them.

Communicating Through Poetry

In earlier chapters you studied the structures which poets create and the sounds and imagery they use. But poetry is more than structure and technical devices; poets write to express their thoughts, feelings, and ideas.

Although poets express their inner feelings through their poems, they also want to communicate those feelings to you. A poet may want to convey a meaning, an insight, or an understanding. A poet may ask you questions that he or she cannot answer. Poetry is not just the poet's isolated expression; it is a shared communication between the poet and you.

Sometimes a poet, such as Gertrude Stein, creates a work that has no identifiable theme but can be appreciated for its sound, imagery, or structure. Yet your enjoyment of a poem often derives from your involvement in the poem. You, as well as the poet, experience its emotions and understand its content and theme.

"From a Childhood": Reading for Meaning

Rainer Maria Rilke's poem evokes a particular moment from a boy's childhood. The beginning of the poem establishes the setting—the interior of a room as daylight fades into darkness. You meet the two characters: a quiet young boy and his mother. When the mother enters the room, she greets her son tenderly. Then the woman sits at the piano and plays a song for her child.

1. Reread the line of dialogue in the poem. Who speaks the line? Explain your answer.

Involving the Reader in the Poem

The real focus of the poem is not the action, but the boy's and the mother's feelings. Although those feelings are never stated directly or described, you understand their intensity. From the first line, the poem evokes a mood that suggests mystery and uneasiness as well as the deep love between mother and son. If you examine the poet's details and descriptions, you will notice how they create the feelings and the mood.

Reread the first two lines of the poem. A boy sits alone in a darkening room. He is "withdrawn and secret." You sense that the room is special to the boy—a safe haven, a secret place of his own.

You also feel that the boy welcomes the darkness. The simile in line 1 suggests why: "The darkening was like riches in the room." The coming of darkness is not threatening; instead, it promises "riches." As the poem unfolds, you learn that the "riches" might be the shared love between mother and son.

2. How does the description in the first two lines involve you in the poem?

In the succeeding lines the boy's world expands to include his mother. As she enters the room, "as in a dream," the mood of mystery and uneasiness deepens. A profound silence fills the room so that only the quivering glass in the cabinet gives her away. She breaks the silence momentarily with her question, but her entrance has been almost as secretive as the boy's presence in the room. Both seem to have escaped for a few moments into this protected haven.

The darkness and the silence support the love between the two characters. Their bond is so strong that both can gaze "timidly towards the piano" and understand each other. Their timid glance is also mysterious, as is the boy's reaction when his mother plays the piano.

3. How is the piano a bond between the boy and his mother?

The poet involves you in his poem by creating an atmosphere of mystery and uncertainty and by revealing an intense moment between a mother and her son. The moment captured in the poem is moving partly because it is communicated in such a simple way. In the first nine lines, the poet develops a series of simple images that combine to create a picture of the room, the boy, his mother, and the piano.

In the last four lines, the picture concentrates on the boy and the object of his gaze—his mother's ringed hand moving across the piano keys.

4. Summarize the images in the final lines. What does the image "all bowed down by the ring" suggest? What mood does it convey?

5. Review the poem. Does the poet effectively communicate his theme? Why or why not?

"Hate is only one of many responses": Reading for Meaning

Frank O'Hara's poem differs from Rilke's in several ways. Instead of telling a story or conveying an emotion, O'Hara's poem is almost like an essay—a piece of prose writing that expresses a person's ideas about certain feelings. Each stanza examines a specific feeling or some aspect of a feeling, just as a new paragraph in an essay might.

6. What feelings does the poem focus on? How do most people view those feelings?

7. What does the speaker urge people to do about those feelings?

Throughout most of the poem, the speaker analyzes and explains the negative feelings that people have. He appears to be addressing his remarks to a general audience. In the last two lines, however, he narrows his audience to one particular person. In those lines he says, if I experience certain negative feelings toward you, they will be "smilingly deflected / by your mysterious concern" for me. That is, if the speaker feels hate, hurt, unkindness, meanness, or selfishness toward the person he is addressing, he will express those feelings. In his relationship with his friend, the speaker knows that the friend will understand him and turn aside the harshness of the speaker's feelings. The other person's "mysterious concern" can withstand the speaker's negative feelings.

8. Think about the last lines of the poem in context with the rest of the poem. What insight into human relationships do they convey?

Communicating Abstract Feelings and Ideas

Many poets, including Frank O'Hara, communicate abstract ideas or feelings. An abstract idea lacks concrete, material qualities such as shape, color, and size. An abstract idea or feeling, such as liberty, justice, or hatred, is hard to define or understand unless it is translated into concrete form.

In "Hate is only one of many responses," O'Hara examines hate, unkindness, meanness, and selfishness, giving each idea form and substance. The speaker talks to you directly and honestly; he does not hide anything. He shares his thoughts, asks questions, and encourages you to act as he suggests. In this way he develops his ideas. In the first few lines the speaker discusses hate, a powerful emotion, but one that should not be feared. Hate, he says, is a natural response even though it can cause pain.

9. Why do "hurt and hate go hand in hand"? Why might a person be "afraid of hate"?

In the second stanza the poet gives hate a concrete form by comparing it to filth. That comparison is another way in which the poet helps you picture hate. Filth is an unpleasant image, whether it is trash blowing around the streets or dust and cobwebs in a room. Yet the speaker says that filth is not really overwhelming and "neither is hate." Is a little dirt really so terrible? Is hate really so bad?

To communicate his ideas about unkindness, the speaker creates two other comparisons. He first says that being unkind is "cleansing"; it is a way of freeing oneself of dirt. Then the speaker offers another comparison: unkindness "allows you to be direct / like an arrow that feels something." With that comparison, he suggests that the truth inevitably involves unkindness. Someone who is direct about his or her true feelings is often considered unkind.

10. Review the comparison between unkindness and the arrow. Why is the comparison effective?

11. How does the speaker feel about meanness?

The speaker is not suggesting that you purposely try to be hateful, unkind, or selfish; he addresses you as a person inclined to be sensitive and understanding. What he is suggesting is that sometimes, especially in close human relationships, people need to deal honestly with the negative feelings that inevitably arise. Those feelings are better acknowledged than ignored or suppressed. You will always feel "a certain reluctance" about such feelings. Most people want to avoid hurting others, especially those they are close to. It is that very reluctance that can make those feelings safe or even valuable, turning them "into gold."

12. Can you think of a situation in which a negative feeling might "turn into gold"? Describe such a situation.

13. Think about the theme of "Hate is only one of many responses." Does the poet effectively communicate that theme? Explain your answer.

Questions for Thought and Discussion

The questions and activities that follow will help you explore the two poems in this chapter in more depth and at the same time develop your critical thinking skills.

1. **Comparing.** Like "From a Childhood," Robert P. Tristram Coffin's poem "The Secret Heart," which you read in Chapter 6, is about a special moment between a parent and a child. Compare the setting, mood, and theme of the two poems.

2. **Expressing an Opinion.** In "Hate is only one of many responses," the speaker urges honesty in a relationship, especially in expressing negative feelings. Do you agree with that view? Under what circumstances might honesty about negative feelings be a bad idea? Do you think complete honesty is always a good idea? Give reasons for your opinion.

3. **Analyzing Details.** Reread "From a Childhood." What details in the poem reveal how the mother feels about her son?

4. **Interpreting.** In stanza 4 of Frank O'Hara's poem, the speaker changes two old sayings. "An ounce of prevention is worth a pound of cure" and "Think of others before yourself" are commonly heard expressions. Why does the speaker change the messages in those sayings?

Writing About Literature

Several suggestions for writing projects are given below. You may be asked to complete one or more of these projects. If you have any questions about how to begin a writing assignment, review Using the Writing Process, beginning on page 219.

1. **Writing a Story About a Character in a Poem.** Think about who the mother and the boy in "From a Childhood" might be, where they might live, and what their lives might be like. Then write a brief story showing some aspect of their lives. For example, you might show them with other members of their family, you might create a dialogue between them, or you might show the boy at school with his friends.

2. **Describing a Setting and a Mood.** Invent a setting that suggests a particular mood. You might, for example, think of a mountainside in autumn when the leaves are changing color. Then describe that setting so that the mood becomes clear. Use imagery, specific details, and figurative language to communicate the setting and the mood to your audience. Have other students in the class identify the mood.

3. **Explaining an Abstract Idea.** Choose an abstract idea such as idealism, happiness, or patriotism. Explain the idea by giving it a concrete form, by using examples, or by making comparisons.

Using the Writing Process

The lesson that follows is designed to help you with the writing assignments you will meet in this book. It explains the major steps in the writing process. Read the lesson carefully so that you understand the writing process thoroughly. On pages 229–230, following the lesson, is a checklist. Whenever you are asked to complete a writing assignment, you can just refer to the checklist as a reminder of the things you should consider as you're working on the assignment. The lesson can then serve as a reference—an information source. Turn to it whenever you feel that it would be helpful to review part or all of the process.

When presented with a writing assignment, many people's instant response is panic. What will I write about? Do I have anything to say? To ease the panic, remind yourself that writing is something that *no one* simply sits down and does with the words flowing freely and perfectly from first sentence to last. Rather, writing is a *process;* that is, it involves a number of steps. The writing process is not a straightforward, mechanical one, such as that involved in solving a mathematical problem. These pages give you a plan that you can follow to sensibly work through the complex task of presenting your ideas on paper.

Keep in mind that writing is not simply the act of filling a piece of paper with words. It is a sophisticated act of communication. The purpose of writing is to put *ideas* across to other people. Since ideas come from your mind, not your pen, the writing process begins with the work that takes place in your mind: the creation and organization of ideas. The process then proceeds to the expression of ideas—the actual setting down of words on paper. The final stage is the polishing of both the ideas and the words that express them.

As they work, writers engage in a variety of activities—thinking, planning, organizing, writing, revising, rethinking. For clarity, we label the various stages in the process prewriting, writing, and revising. However, the stages are not so straightforward and separate. One blends into the next, and sometimes a writer returns to a previous activity, moving back and forth through the process. When you write, your goal should be to produce a clear and lively work that expresses interesting ideas. The writing process can help you in that effort.

Stage 1: Prewriting

Define Your Task

The first stage in the writing process is prewriting. At this stage, your goal is to choose a topic, to figure out what you are going to say about it, and to decide what style and tone you are going to use. Making these decisions is essential if you are going to write something interesting and to express your ideas clearly and vividly. At this stage you jot down thoughts and ideas—the material that you will eventually organize and write about in detail. During the prewriting stage, you should search for answers to the following questions:

What Will I Write About? This question must be answered before you do anything else. You need to choose a topic. Then you need to *focus* the topic. A focused topic directs your thinking as you write. This is important whether you are writing a brief description, a short story, an essay, or a research paper. Deciding just what issues you want to address, what kind of character you want to develop, or what theme and events you want a story to revolve around will focus your thinking and help you create a bright, strong piece of writing.

A careful decision is called for here. A good topic is neither too broad nor too narrow. The length of what you are writing and your purpose for writing often dictate how broad your focus should be. In an essay or a research paper, for instance, you need to choose a topic that's defined enough to explore in depth. You don't want to choose a topic that's so broad that you can only touch on the main ideas. If your assignment is to write a short story, you'll want to focus on perhaps one main relationship between characters, one important conflict, just a few related events. You can then write in detail to create full, interesting characters and a well-developed story. When you need to focus a topic, think about what would be practical for the given task.

What Do I Want to Say? You need to think about what information you want or need to include, and what ideas you want to communicate.

What Is My Purpose for Writing? Will you try to persuade, to inform, to explain, or to entertain your readers?

What Style Will I Use? Do you want to write formally or in a casual, conversational style? Will you use the first person, I, or the third-person, he, she, or they? Will you write seriously or use jokes and humor? If you are writing a story, will you use dialogue?

How Will I Organize My Ideas? What will you start with? In what order will you present and develop your ideas?

Who Is My Audience? Who will be reading your work? Are you writing for other students? For people who already have some background in the subject? For people who know nothing about the subject? For children or for adults? Your audience will dictate the approach you take—whether you will write in a formal or an informal tone, whether you will provide a lot of background information or very little, what kind of words you will use.

Generate and Organize Ideas

Although most of the writing assignments in this book provide fairly specific directions about the type of writing to be done, they leave lots of room for imagination. By using your imagination, you can discover fresh and exciting ideas that are distinctly yours. How can you come up with those bright ideas? Below are some techniques that can help you tap your creative powers. They can help you at the prewriting stage and any time you need to generate new ideas. You might use them to come up with a topic for a research paper, an essay, or a short story. You might use them to focus a topic or to generate ideas about a topic you've already chosen. Techniques such as outlining and clustering are also useful for organizing ideas. Try each of the techniques, and eventually you'll find the ones that work best for you for a particular purpose.

Free Writing. Have you ever been given a writing assignment and found that you had no idea what to write? Free writing is an activity for getting started—for coming up with ideas to write about. To free write, write anything that comes to mind, no matter how far off the topic it seems. At first it may seem silly, but eventually your mind will start associating ideas. Soon you will be writing complete thoughts about the topic.

Suppose you were asked to write about winter. How to begin? Start writing. Put down the first thought that comes to mind and let ideas begin to flow. You might come up with something like this:

> I don't know what to write. Winter. What can I say that hasn't already been said about winter? It's cold, there's lots of snow . . . well, not in all places I guess. Actually when it's cold here, it's warm on the other side of the world. Do they call that winter then, or summer . . . ?

Can you see how you might go from thoughts that are totally off the track to thoughts that are intriguing? When you have finished, look at all the ideas you've written down. Perhaps there are whole sentences or paragraphs that can go into your story or essay. This exercise will have gotten you started.

Brainstorming. This also is an activity to generate ideas. It can be done alone or in a group. When brainstorming, you want to come up with as many ideas as possible. Each idea will spur a new idea. As you or others in a brainstorming group think of ideas, write them down. After you have come up with all the ideas you can, select several to develop for the assignment.

Clustering. This technique can be useful both to generate ideas and to organize them. In fact, you actually do both at the same time, for as you jot down ideas, you "cluster" the ones that go together.

Begin by putting your main idea—your focused topic—in the center of the page and circling it. As you think of ideas associated with the main idea, write them nearby, circle them, and connect them with a line to the main idea. Then, as you think of ideas related to each of those *subtopics*, attach the ideas to the word they relate to. You can take this process as far as you like. The farther you branch out, the more detailed you get. When you get to the point where you're ready to write your story or your essay, you can use such a diagram as a guide to grouping your ideas. A simple clustering diagram is shown below. The main idea is "symbols in a story."

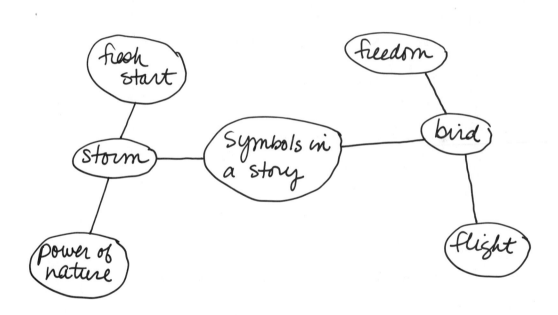

Outlining. Outlining is usually thought of as an organizing tool, but it also provides a useful form in which to write down ideas as you think of them. It gives you a way to group ideas, just as clustering does. In addition, it helps you

Using the Writing Process

to organize those groups of ideas—to arrange them in the order in which you think you would like to write about them.

Start by writing down some main ideas that you want to include. Leave space after each one for listing related facts or thoughts—details—that you will want to include about the topic. Each idea you list will probably make you think of another idea. Look at the example below. Imagine that your assignment is to write a character sketch. You think you'd like to write about an old man. That's a main idea, so you write it down. One of the aspects of the man you want to talk about is his lifestyle. That, too, is a main idea, so you leave some space after your first idea and write it down. Okay, you ask yourself, what is the old man like? List each specific detail under the first main idea. Go on and do the same with lifestyle, and whatever other main ideas you may have.

Character Sketch

Old Man
 about 80 years old
 tall, thin, straight
 athletic
 friendly, outgoing

Man's Lifestyle
 lives in his own apartment in the city
 involved in theater
 many friends of all ages

You can work back and forth in an outline, adding and deleting, until you're satisfied with the ideas that are there. Your last step will be to arrange the outline in the order in which you think you want to present the ideas in your writing. Then the outline becomes a kind of map for writing. Remember, though, that it's a loose map—you can rearrange, drop, and add ideas even as you are writing.

Outlining is also a good way of organizing the ideas you generate through brainstorming and free writing. It helps you place those ideas in some kind of order.

Stage 2: Writing

The second stage in the writing process is the writing itself. At this stage, you write a first draft of your paper or story, using the notes or outline that you developed in the prewriting stage as a guide. This is the stage at which you turn those loose ideas into sentences and paragraphs that work together.

Get Your Thoughts on Paper. When you begin writing, the most important thing to focus on is saying what you want to say—getting all your ideas down on paper in sentences and paragraphs. Some people find it easiest to write their first drafts without worrying if they have chosen exactly the right words and without checking on spelling. Just put a question mark next to anything you aren't sure of and check it later. You can even put a blank in a sentence if you can't think of the right word to put there. Fill it in when you revise.

As you are writing, you may discover that you sometimes have to go back and do some more thinking and planning. You may need to gather more information or think through an idea again. You may also do some rearranging of ideas.

Develop a Tone. In the writing stage, you need to begin to develop a tone— an attitude toward your subject. How do you want to *sound* to the reader? What impression do you want the reader to have toward the subject? Do you want to sound authoritative, amusing, sad, pleased? You'll want to establish your tone right away—in the first paragraph. The first paragraph is important because it must grab your reader's interest and show where you are headed.

Organize Your Writing. As you write, you will, of course, be following the basic rules of the language. Sentences should express complete thoughts. They should follow one another in logical order. Each paragraph should focus on one main idea, and it should contain details that support that idea.

As you move from one paragraph to the next, use transition words and phrases to link your ideas. Clearly connect ideas and thoughts that go together so the reader can follow your story, argument, or explanation.

Stage 3: Revising

The third stage in the writing process is revising. This is the point at which you look for ways to polish your writing. Revising is more than just fixing a few errors. It can involve both major and minor changes.

Rethink Ideas and Organization

The first goal in revising is to check for clear, logical expression. Does what I have written make sense? Have I clearly said everything I am trying to say? Have I arranged my ideas in the best order?

Reread the entire draft to see if paragraphs and sentences follow in a logical order. You may find that putting paragraphs in a different order makes your points clearer. Remember that each paragraph is part of a whole, and it should relate to your topic. Sometimes you may write an excellent paragraph, only to discover that it has very little to do with the topic. No matter how good you think a sentence or a paragraph is, drop it if it doesn't belong.

As you read what you have written, you may also want to rewrite sentences and paragraphs, or even add new material. At this stage, you may also want to go back to your prewriting notes to see that you included everything you wanted to include.

Look at Your Language

After you have checked the ideas and organization, review the style and form in which you have written. Think about the language—the words and phrases you have used. Do they say precisely what you mean? Do they create strong images?

If you want your writing to be lively and interesting, write with strong verbs and nouns. They make strong writing. If you find yourself piling on the adjectives and adverbs, you'll know that you're struggling to support weak verbs and nouns. What is a strong verb or noun? It is one that is precise, active, fresh. It paints a clear picture in the mind.

Use Strong Verbs. Some verbs, for instance, are tired, overused, dull. The verb *to be*, for example, is about the weakest verb in the language. It doesn't *do* anything. So look at the sentences in which you use the verbs *is, are, am, was, have been*, etc. Are there action words that you can use instead? Instead of saying "Sam was happy," might you describe an action that *shows* that Sam was happy? "Sam smiled shyly and nodded his head," "Sam beamed," "Sam grinned," "Sam jumped into the air, arms raised above his head, and shouted, YES!"

Use Precise Nouns. Your nouns too should be precise. Whenever possible, create a strong image for the reader. The word *thing*, for instance, is imprecise and overused. What kind of image does it create in your mind? None. Search for the word that *tells*. If you are describing a street scene, for instance, instead of saying that there is a building on the corner, can you tell what kind of building it is? Is it a bank? A three-story Victorian house? A gothic cathedral? An open-air vegetable market? Draw clear pictures with your nouns.

Don't Overuse Adjectives and Adverbs. Adjectives and adverbs have their place, but try not to overdo them. When you do find yourself in need of an adjective, choose one that creates a strong image. Avoid those that are overused and don't really describe. *Beautiful* and *nice*, for instance, are overused adjectives.

Toss Out Unnecessary Words. Have you used more words than you need to say something? This is known as being redundant. Saying that someone is "bright and intelligent," for instance, is redundant because the adjectives are synonyms. Use one or the other. Another example is the phrase "crucially important." Why not just say "crucial"?

As you examine your language, throw out any words that don't serve a purpose—that don't give information, paint a clear picture, create atmosphere. By taking out unnecessary words, you will have "tight writing"—writing that moves along.

Check the Structure and Rhythm of Your Sentences. Read your work out loud and listen to the rhythm and sounds of the language. Do the sentences all sound the same? If they do, can you vary the structure of your sentences— making some simple, some complex, some long, some short? Correct any sentence fragments, and divide run-on sentences into two or more sentences.

After you've gone through that kind of thinking a few times at the revision stage, you'll find yourself automatically choosing livelier, clearer language as you write. You'll become a better writer. That, too, is a process.

Check for Errors

The final step in the revising process is the all-important "housekeeping" review—checking for correct spelling, grammar, and punctuation, and for readable handwriting. You don't, of course, have to wait until the end of the writing process to pay attention to those details. But before you write your final draft, check carefully for errors in those areas.

Checklist for the Writing Process

✓ What is my topic? Is it focused enough? Should I broaden or narrow it?

✓ What do I want to say about the topic? What are my thoughts, feelings, and ideas about it?

✓ Which prewriting activity or activities would most help me to gather ideas?

✓ Do I need to do some research? Some reading? Consult outside sources? What other materials, if any, do I need?

✓ What is the main point or idea that I want to communicate? What ideas are secondary? Which of those ideas are most important?

✓ What details will I include to support and expand on the main ideas?

✓ Should I include examples or anecdotes?

✓ How will I organize my ideas?

✓ What is my purpose for writing? Do I want to entertain? Inform? Explain? Persuade? Perhaps a combination?

✓ Who is my audience?

✓ What kind of language will I use? Will I be formal, informal, or casual? Will I use dialogue? Will I speak directly to the reader?

✓ What tone do I want to take—what feeling do I want to give the reader about the subject? How can I sustain that tone throughout my writing?

✓ How can I effectively begin my first paragraph? Should I use a question? A startling or unusual fact? An amazing statistic? Should I begin with an action or a description? Perhaps a piece of dialogue?

✓ How will I end? If writing nonfiction, should I summarize what I have already said, or should I offer a new thought or argument as my conclusion?

✓ Have I developed my ideas in the best order possible? Should I move some paragraphs around?

✓ Have I covered my topic adequately? Does the writing fulfill its purpose and get the main point across to my audience?

✓ Do I need to rewrite parts? Perhaps some ideas need to be clarified or explained further. Perhaps I could write a better description or account of an event?

✓ Do I want to add anything?

✓ Are there any unnecessary ideas or details that should be deleted?

✓ Is each paragraph well developed—are the facts and ideas presented in a good order?

✓ Do all the sentences in each paragraph relate to one idea?

✓ Are the ideas between sentences and between paragraphs connected with transition words and phrases that make the connections clear?

✓ Is the writing vivid? Have I used active, precise, colorful words that create strong images?

✓ Does the final paragraph provide a good ending?

✓ Are the sentences well constructed? Are there any run-ons or sentence fragments that need fixing? Do I vary the kinds of sentences—some long, some short, some active, some passive?

✓ Is the grammar correct?

✓ Are all the words spelled correctly?

✓ Is all the punctuation correct?

✓ Is the final draft clean and legible?

✓ Have I read the final draft over one last time to check for any errors that may have crept in as I was copying?

Glossary of Literary Terms

This glossary includes definitions for all the important literary terms introduced in this book. The first time they are defined and discussed in the text, the terms are underlined. Following each term in the glossary is a page reference (in parentheses) that tells the page on which the term is introduced.

Many terms are discussed in more than one chapter, especially as they apply to various selections. This glossary provides the fullest definition of each term. Boldfaced words within the definitions are other terms that appear in the glossary.

alliteration (page 37) the close **repetition** of the same first sounds in words, usually consonant sounds. Poets use alliteration to add emphasis to an idea or to certain words, or to heighten the **mood** of a line or a **stanza.** Although alliteration usually occurs at the beginnings of words, it can also occur within words.

allusion (page 103) a reference to something real or fictitious outside of the poem.

analogy (page 160) a comparison that demonstrates the similarities between two things.

assonance (page 38) the **repetition** of similar vowel sounds within words to emphasize certain sounds and add a musical quality.

ballad (page 172) a song that tells a simple story. Many ballads have been passed from generation to generation by word of mouth before being written down. Most ballads are written in four-line **stanzas.** Many ballads contain **epithets** and a **refrain.**

broadside ballad (page 172) a **ballad** composed to address a current event or issue.

calligramme (page 146) a poem designed by Guillaume Apollinaire in which the arrangement of the typography, or printed letters, helps to convey the meaning. *See* **concrete poetry.**

conceit (page 161) an elaborate and detailed **metaphor** that compares two very different objects or situations. Although the comparison may initially seem farfetched, a conceit actually reveals precision, clarity, and logic.

concrete language (page 71) words that describe things that the reader knows and understands with his or her senses. Concrete language describes something that actually exists and can be seen or touched in the reader's mind. *See* **image.**

concrete poetry (page 146) poetry that conveys meaning through its visual shape on the page. *See* **calligramme.**

connotation (page 50) the emotion that a word arouses or the meanings it suggests beyond its **denotation,** or dictionary meaning.

denotation (page 50) the dictionary meaning of a word.

dialogue (page 123) the actual conversation between the characters.

diction (page 36) a poet's choice and arrangement of words.

end rhyme (page 16) the **repetition** of syllable sounds that occurs at the ends of lines of poetry. *See* **rhyme scheme.**

epithet (page 183) a descriptive word or phrase that expresses a quality or characteristic of an object or a person. An epithet is often used in place of the name of a person or thing. The epithet "Lion-Hearted" is commonly used for Richard I of England, who is referred to as Richard the Lion-Hearted.

feminine rhyme (page 17) rhyming words that consist of a stressed syllable followed by one or more unstressed syllables. A feminine rhyme in "Annabel Lee," by Edgar Allan Poe, occurs with the words *chilling* and *killing*. *See* **masculine rhyme** and **stress.**

figurative language (page 86) words and phrases used in unusual ways to create strong, vivid **images,** to focus attention on certain ideas, and to compare things that are basically different. When words or phrases are used figuratively, they have meanings other than their usual, or literal, meanings. *See* specific **figures of speech** such as **metaphor, personification,** and **simile.**

figure of speech (page 86) a word or phrase that creates a vivid **image** by contrasting unlike things. A figure of speech has meanings other than its ordinary meaning.

flashback (page 124) a scene, a conversation, or an event that interrupts the present action to show something that has happened in the past.

foot (page 20) the unit in which **meter** is counted. A foot consists of one stressed syllable and its one or more unstressed syllables. The number of feet in a line of poetry equals the number of stressed syllables. *See* **scanning** and **stress.**

free verse (page 62) a poem that does not have any fixed **meter, rhyme,** or line length. The verse is called "free" because the poet is free to change the patterns or to use no pattern at all. Much twentieth-century poetry is written in free verse.

haiku (page 62) a brief, highly structured poem composed of seventeen syllables broken into three lines of five, seven, and five syllables. In a haiku the poet lightly sketches an experience by concentrating on a single, central **image.**

homonym (page 53) a word that is pronounced like another word but has a different spelling and meaning, such as *write* and *right.*

iambic pentameter (page 20) a five-foot line in which each **foot** is an iamb. In English poetry iambic pentameter is used more often than any other **meter.**

image (page 18) a word or phrase that creates a mental picture of something for the reader. Although most images are visual, an image can appeal to any of the senses—sight, sound, taste, smell, and touch. *See* **imagery.**

imagery (page 63) all the **images** that are created in a poem.

implicit metaphor (page 88) a special kind of **metaphor** in which one of the terms is not stated but suggested by the context. "The children flocked to the ice cream stand" is an example of an implicit metaphor in which the children are indirectly compared to sheep by the word *flocked*. See **figurative language.**

internal rhyme (page 16) **rhyme** that occurs when a word within a line rhymes with another word in the line.

light verse (page 171) poetry that uses an ordinary speaking voice and a relaxed manner to treat its subject cheerfully, comically, or with ridicule.

lyric poem (page 129) poetry that has a single **speaker** and expresses a deeply felt thought or emotion. The speaker does not have a specific audience; that is, the speaker seems to be addressing himself or herself.

masculine rhyme (page 17) rhyming words of one stressed syllable. An example of masculine rhyme in "Annabel Lee," by Edgar Allan Poe, occurs with the words *sea* and *Lee*. See **feminine rhyme** and **stress.**

metaphor (page 87) an implied comparison between unlike things. A metaphor is a comparison that suggests one thing *is* another. The purpose of a metaphor is to give the reader an unusual way of looking at one of the things. *See* **figurative language.**

metaphysical conceit (page 161) a **conceit** that creates parallels between the spiritual qualities of an idea and a physical object.

meter (page 19) the regular pattern of stressed and unstressed syllables in a line of poetry. Meter is counted in feet. The most common meter in English poetry is **iambic pentameter.** *See* **foot** and **stress.**

mood (page 17) the general feeling or atmosphere created in a poem.

narrative poem (page 129) poetry that tells a story. The story may be true or imagined.

paradox (page 161) a statement that appears to be self-contradictory or untrue, but which actually reveals a truth.

parody (page 181) a type of humorous writing in which a writer ridicules a serious literary subject.

personification (page 89) a **figure of speech** in which an animal, an object, or an idea is given human qualities. Poets often use personification to describe abstract ideas such as freedom, truth, and beauty. *See* **figurative language.**

quatrain (page 90) a four-line **stanza.** The quatrain is a very common form in English poetry.

refrain (page 16) one or more lines that are repeated regularly throughout a poem. A refrain is often found in a **ballad.**

repetition (page 15) the reappearance of a sound, a word, a phrase, or a line in a poem.

rhyme (page 16) the **repetition** of the same or similar sound or sounds. Rhyme is often related to meaning because it brings two or more words together.

rhyme scheme (page 18) the pattern of **end rhyme** in a poem. A poem has a rhyme scheme when the words at the ends of two or more lines rhyme. Rhyme scheme adds to the musical sound of poetry and can affect the **mood** of the poem. The rhyme scheme of a poem can be shown by assigning a different letter of the alphabet to each line-end sound in a **stanza.** Lines that rhyme are given the same letter. For example, if the first and second lines have one rhyme and the third and fourth lines have another, the rhyme scheme would be *aabb.*

rhythm (page 19) the pattern of stressed and unstressed syllables in a poem. Through rhythm, a poet can highlight the musical quality of language. Rhythm can serve other purposes, such as emphasizing ideas or making actions more vivid. The standard way of showing the rhythm of a poem is by using symbols: [∕] for a stressed syllable, and [∪] for an unstressed syllable. *See* **stress.**

scanning (page 20) counting the feet, or number and arrangement of stressed and unstressed syllables in a line, to determine the **meter.** *See* **foot** and **stress.**

simile (page 86) a direct comparison between unlike things that are connected by *like, as,* or *resembles* or the verb *appears* or *seems.* The purpose of a simile is to give the reader a vivid new way of looking at one of the things. *See* **figurative language.**

sonnet (page 89) a fourteen-line poem with a fixed pattern of **rhythm** and **meter.** The lines are usually in **iambic pentameter.**

speaker (page 15) the voice that talks in a poem. The speaker may or may not reflect the poet's voice. The speaker may be a character that the poet has created and may even be an animal or an object.

stanza (page 16) a group of lines that forms a section of the poem. Each stanza often has the same **rhyme** pattern.

stress (page 17) words or syllables that receive greater accent, or emphasis, than others. Stress gives a word or syllable greater force or prominence in a line of poetry.

structure (page 131) the poet's arrangement or overall design of a work. In poetry structure refers to the way the words and lines are arranged to produce a particular effect.

suspense (page 183) the interest, excitement, and anticipation the reader feels about what will happen in the poem.

symbol (page 102) a person, a place, or an object that stands for something other or more important than itself.

synonym (page 53) a word having practically the same meaning as another word, such as *car* and *auto.*

theme (page 53) the underlying message of a piece of writing.

tone (page 124) a poet's attitude toward his or her subject, audience, or self.

verse paragraph (page 145) a group of lines in a poem that forms a unit similar to that of a prose paragraph. The lines need not be formally arranged in a **stanza.**